TIME AND THE ART OF LIVING

TITIAN: ALLEGORY OF PRUDENCE
(*London: National Gallery*)

TIME AND THE ART OF LIVING

ROBERT GRUDIN

TICKNOR & FIELDS NEW YORK

Copyright © 1982 by Robert Grudin

ALL RIGHTS RESERVED

For information about permission to reproduce selections from this
book, write to Permissions, Harper & Row, Publishers, Inc.,
10 East 53rd Street, New York, New York 10017.

The frontispiece illustration is reproduced
by courtesy of the Trustees,
The National Gallery,
London.

Library of Congress Cataloging-in-Publication Data

Grudin, Robert.
Time and the art of living / Robert Grudin.
p. cm.
Reprint. Originally published: Cambridge, Mass. : Harper & Row, c1982.
ISBN 0-89919-789-2 (pbk.)
1. Time.   2. Conduct of life.   I. Title.
[BD638.G75 1988]
115 — dc19   88-10098
CIP

Printed in the United States of America

D 10 9 8 7 6 5 4 3 2 1

Ticknor & Fields paperback 1988

For
JOSEPHINE DUVENECK
In Memoriam

CLOYCE DUNCAN
HANS SPEIER

ANTHONY GRUDIN
NICHOLAS GRUDIN
THEODORE GRUDIN
MICHAELA GRUDIN

How sour sweet music is
When time is broke, and no proportion kept!
So is it in the music of men's lives.
And here have I the daintiness of ear
To check time broke in a disordered string;
But for the concord of my state and time
Had not an ear to hear my true time broke.
I wasted time, and now doth time waste me.

Shakespeare, *Richard II*
(act 5, scene 5, lines 42–49)

❧ CONTENTS ❧

❧ *PREFACE* ❧

Time is everywhere, yet eludes us. Time is so bound up in our universe and ourselves that it resists our efforts to isolate and define it. Time haunts our experience like some invisible spirit of things, some irretrievable truth. And when we try to manage our own time, setting new goals, cleaning and rearranging the little houses of our days, time gently mocks us — not so much because we lack wit as because time operates on a deeper psychological level than conscious effort can normally reach. This book does not attempt to isolate or organize time. Instead it attempts, on the broadest possible scale, to do justice to time's rooted coherence in nature. My premise, which is quite traditional, is that the acceptance and appreciation of nature are the only channels to its elusive bounty, the only valid foundations of boldness and achievement. My approach has two corollaries, which together explain the unusual format of this book. First, since time refused to sit still for my portrait, I have written instead a kind of moving picture, a series of statements and reflections which readers may follow at their own pace. Rather than leading readers to preordained conclusions, I wish to make them stop and think. Rather than pretending to consistency and connectedness, I wish to set off an autonomous interplay of comparisons and contrasts. The blank spaces between my writings are as important as the writings themselves. Second, since time operates most dramatically on our dearest values and concerns, I have been unable to avoid making statements about these matters; so that what began as an objective discourse on time has ended up as a personal philosophy of life. For this unavoidable excess I take full responsibility, trusting that readers will sort out what is valuable from what is not, and that those who find nothing of value will forgive and forget.

TIME AND THE ART OF LIVING

I ✦ A PROSPECT
OF TIME ✦✦✦✦

1.1 ✦ IN A RAILROAD CAR AT NIGHTFALL, WHEN the natural light outside has diminished until it is even with the artificial light inside, the passenger facing forward sees in his window two images at once: the dim landscape rushing toward him out of a pit of darkness, and the interior of the car, reflected with its more or less motionless occupants. At this hour most passengers unconsciously give allegiance to one of these two polarities of vision; and the individual momentarily aware of both may be struck by the profound, almost tragic duality between outer and inner worlds, between the rush of experience and the immobility of awareness. The uneasy contrast implied by this image is to my mind one of the special marks of our condition, one of the tragic divorces between our lonely humanity and the pulse of nature.

1.2 ✦ BUT THIS DIVORCE NEED NOT BE TOTAL OR final. The runner, covering the same route again and again, comes to think of that route as something which, transcending mere geography, is a kind of space-time. That long level tree-lined stretch, inseparable in the mind from virtuous thoughts and breathing difficulties, is half a mile *and* four minutes — and neither one without the other. We might consider this a temporary coincidence of concerns, a dimensional confusion brought on by physical strain. But more likely the mind and body are winning their way to

a valid and dignified level of reality, discovering a unified phenomenology which, though omnipresent, is seldom seen or felt.

More abstractly, the use of metaphor — temporal metaphor for
space and spatial metaphor for time — gives us a special sort of
access to the space-time continuum. This is not because metaphor
has anything particular to do with the physics of space-time, but
rather because metaphor evokes both conscious and subconscious
responses and produces, more fully than do logic or common sense,
an awareness of the implicit connectedness of things.

1.3 ✍ LIKE STUDENTS OF ART WHO WALK AROUND
a great statue, seeing parts and aspects of it from each position, but
never the whole work, we must walk mentally around time, using
a variety of approaches, a pandemonium of metaphor. No insight
or association, however outlandish or contradictory, should be forbidden us; the only thing forbidden should be to stand still and
say, "This is it."

1.4 ✍ FAST DRIVERS CAN SEE NO FURTHER THAN
slow drivers, but they must look further down the road to time
their reactions safely. Similarly, people with great projects afoot
habitually look further and more clearly into the future than people who are mired in day-to-day concerns. These former control
the future because by necessity they must project themselves into
it; and the upshot is that, like ambitious settlers, they stake out
larger plots and homesteads of time than the rest of us. They do
not easily grow sad or old; they are seldom intimidated by the
alarms and confusions of the present because they have something
greater of their own, some sense of their large and coherent motion in time, to compare the present with.

1.5 ✍ THE EXTENT TO WHICH WE LIVE FROM
day to day, from week to week, intent on details and oblivious to
larger presences, is a gauge of our impoverishment in time. We

drive through long stretches of magnificent country, less with pleasure than anxiety and fatigue, and come away bearing only the jumbled images of stop signs, passing lanes and gas stations. Deprived of the continuum, we lose not only the sole valid alternative to a present-centered existence but also the nourishing context which can give substance and value to the present itself.

1.6 ✍ PSYCHOLOGICALLY TIME IS SELDOM homogeneous but rather is as full of shapes as space. Like the stress lines in metal or the patterns of ocean currents, these shapes become visible only when subjected to certain forms of analysis, but are invaluable in determining the nature of the thing studied. For example, time as we know it generally divides itself into threes. Every definite period, from an hour's wait in an airport to a year's sojourn abroad, resolves itself into beginning, middle and end — natural divisions of radically distinct character. Time runs slower at the beginning, faster at the end of a period; for we tend to conceive of periods in terms of time remaining rather than time elapsed, and minutes near the end of a period constitute a greater percentage of remaining time than minutes near the beginning. Time at the beginnings and ends of periods is generally fragmented. We sit down to read for two hours and spend the first few minutes arranging ourselves in our chairs, stationing our lamps and generally trying to free our minds from the immediate past and burrow them into present concentration. A hundred-odd minutes later our concentration begins to flag. We look at our watches more frequently, stretch stiff muscles, and deal with the anticipation or anxiety which inheres in the activity to come. It is at the center of the period, distinct from these two extremes but protected by them, that the heart of the activity and the real value of the involvement lie. Two obvious corollaries spring from these principles: (1) In planning ahead we should remember that usable time is at best 80 to 85 percent of total time. (2) Long unbroken periods contain more usable time than do short periods totaling the same length.

1.7 ✍ ENCLOSURES LOOK SMALL UNTIL WE ARE within them. Cottages look tiny from the outside; and newly framed houses, in the absurdly limitless context of outdoor space, seem puny and shrunken. But once they are properly walled in and we are properly inside them, they no longer seem small. Through the eye, the mind has adjusted from vacant space to human space — from a context in which human stature is meaningless to one in which it has significance; and the rooms seem large enough. A similar metamorphosis is possible in time. If we view time as amorphous and homogeneous, we simply swim our way through days and weeks; we barely exist in time, for our wayfaring awareness is lost in its huge scale. But if we roof and wall time into chambers of expectation, plan and commitment, our days become memorable. Time takes on significance when we frame it on a human scale.

1.8 🖎 THE MOSQUE AT CÓRDOBA IS A RELATIVELY low building with an immense floor area. The interior is one great dimly-lit chamber punctuated by a thousand Moorish columns in long, even rows. To an observer standing at or near the middle of the room, these columns seem to stretch endlessly, as parallels or diagonals, in all directions, like trees in a great orchard (in fact, this arrangement is duplicated by the orange trees in the courtyard outside). The feeling of being lost among these graceful forms and isolated from other realities is strangely pleasant — a happy surrender of spatial context and identity — and is not unlike the feeling of being pleasurably lost in time, deep in the luscious monotony of a country holiday or the long minutes of a summer day. In time as well as space, the surrender of specific being turns out to be no loss at all, but rather the only way of expanding into a grander and more general form of being — a heroic being whose characteristics, though deeply familiar to all of us, are seldom available in everyday life. To appreciate the full dimensions of space or time, we cannot merely sample them, but must voyage into them, lose ourselves in them, expand within their vastness.

1.9 🖎 LIKE A MACHINE WHICH SORTS OUT A great variety of objects into individually homogeneous bundles, time sorts and garners up our various productions. We smoke only one cigarette at a time, but in a few years our lungs look as though we had inhaled a volcano. We experience isolated moments of affection and delight, and find in a few weeks that we are in love. We tell lies in order to deliver ourselves from particular emergencies, yet soon discover that we are on a generally false footing. We jot down, from day to day, individual perceptions, and are ultimately visited by unified ideas. Yet we seldom think of the specific phenomena as parts of a coherent whole. Time plays the big arpeggios of victory and defeat, achievement, disaffection, the whole gamut; but we hear only the single tones. And in missing the incremental structure, the temporal coherence of our lives, we miss the truth about ourselves.

Free men and women, on the other hand, can think across time, viewing their own lives, inclusive of past, present and future, as architectural wholes, static in mental space. They can therefore see, as others cannot, the cracks and buttresses of repeated action, the points of stress, the established framework. They are not perfect; but they are less imperfect than we by a full dimension of being.

To approach freedom of this sort, we must begin with a single simple thought, addressable to almost any of our daily actions, but particularly pertinent to moral choices: "I have done this before, I will do it again."

1.10 ✒ EARLY MORNINGS OR LATE AFTERNOONS in the country offer wonderful dualities of light. You can look down-light (away from the sun) and see placid outlines of nature, smooth, distinct and flattened into repose. The old light bouncing back at you organizes the landscape and gives every view the aspect of something specially prepared. You can look up-light for startling revolutions of brightness and shadow, leaves filled with exuberant orange radiance, glimpses of unspecified golden promise. So in the same moment there are two seasons, and you can glance back and forth at visions deeply suggestive of past and future.

1.11 ✒ ROOMS CAN BE VESSELS OF PSYCHOLOGICAL temporality, silently encouraging specific attitudes toward time:

The furniture of the past: shelved books, dried flowers, windows facing west, antiques, old photographs and paintings, lamplight, miscellaneous articles, complicated space.

The furniture of the present: chairs and tables chosen for utility, a bowl of fruit, an open book, current periodicals, windows to the south, overhead lights, cut flowers or potted plants, modern art, mirrors.

The furniture of the future: bare walls, a skylight, windows facing east, much open space, a barometer, clear desk, sharpened pencils, blank pad, unopened book, unopened bottle of wine, skylights, light colors, large doorless openings to other rooms.

I.12 ✍ IN LATE NOVEMBER OF 1968, I SPENT A few days in a hotel just off the Piazza San Marco in Venice. At 6 one morning, hearing the loud warning bells, I jumped out of bed, grabbed my camera and rushed out to see the famous Venetian flood. I stood in the empty and as yet dry Piazza and looked out toward the Gulf, for I expected the flood tides to come in from the open water. Many minutes passed before I turned to see that the Piazza was flooding, not directly from the Gulf, but up through its own sewers. The indented gratings in the pavement had all but disappeared under calm, flat silver puddles, which grew slowly and silently until their peripheries touched and the Piazza had become a lake. That morning I experienced vividly, if almost subliminally, the reality of change itself: how it fools our sentinels and undermines our defenses, how careful we are to look for it in the wrong places, how it does not reveal itself until it is beyond redress, how vainly we search for it around us and find too late that it has occurred within us.

I.13 ✍ OUR COMMON IMAGE OF EXPERIENCE IS about as accurate as a still photograph of a man riding a bicycle. Project this image back into reality, and the man will fall off his bicycle.

1.14 ✍ IMAGINE THAT YOU SPENT YOUR WHOLE life at a single house. Each day at the same hour you entered an artificially-lit room, undressed and took up the same position in front of a motion picture camera. It photographed one frame of you per day, every day of your life. On your seventy-second birthday, the reel of film was shown. You saw yourself growing and aging over seventy-two years in less than half an hour (27.4 minutes at sixteen frames per second). Images of this sort, though terrifying, are helpful in suggesting unfamiliar but useful perspectives of time. They may, for example, symbolize the telescoped, almost momentary character of the past as seen through the eyes of an anxious or disaffected individual. Or they may suggest the remarkable brevity of our lives in the cosmic scale of time. If the estimated age of the cosmos were shortened to seventy-two years, a human life would take about ten seconds.

But look at time the other way. Each day is a minor eternity of over 86,000 seconds. During each second, the number of distinct molecular functions going on within the human body is comparable to the number of seconds in the estimated age of the cosmos. A few seconds are long enough for a revolutionary idea, a startling communication, a baby's conception, a wounding insult, a sudden death. Depending on how we think of them, our lives can be infinitely long or infinitely short.

1.15 ✍ GREAT DRAMA, LIKE THE ENERGY implicit in every atom, is eternally around us and within us, but liberated only by coincidence, ceremony, creativity, periods reaching completion, pressures reaching the bursting point, and the simple but painful cultivation of awareness.

1.16 ✍ WE CAN OFTEN, EVEN AT A GLANCE, SEE an object's extension in time. Imagine a hillside of oaks and wildflowers, or a page of newsprint blown by the wind down a street of old brownstones, or a camper's tent under a granite cliff. In each of these images, an extreme contrast between the visually-perceived nature of two objects suggests an equally extreme contrast between their hypothetical extensions in time — here, between relative impermanence and relative permanence. When we recognize contrasts of this kind, we are in a fashion *seeing time*, perceiving the dimension which comprehends the other three and gives them meaning.

Other examples could be multiplied. A paperback has a temporal extension different from that of a hardbound book, a cedar chest from one of plywood, a stone wall from a picket fence. Even phenomena of a strongly temporal nature — a wedding or a baptism or a funeral — extend themselves in our sense of time differently from other phenomena — a baseball game, cocktail party or committee meeting. Perceptions of all these phenomena constantly excite our temporal faculties; though we are often less than fully conscious of these faculties or their significance. Our goal should be to make these processes more conscious — to refine and unify our sixth sense of time.

1.17 ✒ FOUR-DIMENSIONALITY SUGGESTS new forms of symmetry and asymmetry. Objects or events that seem perfectly compact and well-proportioned in space can be rendered four-dimensionally flat or narrow or oblong by their unusual extensions in time. The difference, for example, between a cloud and a pebble, or between a fat Sunday newspaper and a Shakespeare sonnet, is the difference between phenomena which are large spatially but small temporally and phenomena which are small spatially but large temporally. Speaking more generally, we could say that small things are noticed only when they last, brief things only when they are massive or voluminous. These gross distinctions in four-dimensional proportion suggest that a mean may exist: a class of phenomena that are symmetrical in space-time. What sort of things would these be? One thinks of the face and the planetary system of Jupiter, a rainbow, a stand of mature redwoods, the Parthenon. This exclusive order of objects, which seem to *be* in time exactly what they are in space, have a special meaning. Perhaps our sense of symmetry in space-time is cognate with our sense of beauty.

1.18 ✍ UNLESS WE ARE CAREFUL, WE TEND TO slip into an attitude toward time which is rather like that of a passenger who sits facing backward on a speeding train. The present (such objects as can be seen by looking out at a 90-degree angle to the direction of the train) passes in a blur, like matter without form. Once past, they take on a momentary appearance of three-dimensionality, an evanescent illusion of integrity in themselves and coherence with each other. But long before we can appreciate them or draw conclusions from them, they are gone; other objects replace them; all inject themselves inexorably into the vague placid huddle, the matterless form, of the distant background. Fixing our eyes on this background in hopes of finding something stable and dependable, we notice that it too is changing. But here the cheat is not speed but rather slowness: we are baffled by alterations too subtle to pinpoint but too profound to ignore. Present consciousness, therefore, and memory, are tantalizing but useless; past and present glow with a meaning which our habitual attitude cannot unlock. We sense that the future might give reality and meaning to everything, but it is dark and empty to us, walled off by a seemingly windowless physical barrier. It mystifies us, tempts us, almost nags us; yet in fear and confusion we look for it everywhere but where it is. For the real problem of time is not in nature but rather in our position toward nature, not in what we see but in the way we look.

1.19 ✍ IN OLD MAGAZINES AND NEWSPAPERS WE find a number of uncomfortably revealing things: the aged as young, the dead as living, forgotten people as celebrities, an array of our own barbarous and long-discarded fads and postures, and worst, visible only in this removed perspective, our own sickening pretensions to meaning and permanence.

1.20 ✍ GREAT ATHLETES SEEM TO OPERATE ON a different level of time from that inhabited by lesser mortals. Specifically, they seem to be able to integrate more action into the present, to do a greater number of things at the same time or during a given period of time. Sugar Ray Robinson claimed, without notable disagreement from his opponents, that he could see the opening and throw the punch simultaneously. Another middle-weight champion, Nino Benvenuti, once threw a knockout punch and had his arm raised in triumph before his opponent touched the canvas. Muhammad Ali could "hook off a jab," making a heavy punch unexpectedly materialize out of the same hand which had only just delivered a light one. Longer time periods give occasion for even more surprising mastery. Ilie Nastase, who at his best gave the impression less that he was competing at tennis than working out (with his opponent as apprentice) the full possibilities of an art form, was once described by a perceptive reporter as having "manufactured" time. This remark referred to an unusual combination of talents in action: concentration, balance, speed, quickness, coordination, reflex, anticipation, providence and control of tempo. Just as a tennis player who has mastered the full repertoire of shots has more court to use and literally sees the in-bounds surface as a larger area than that seen by the common hacker, Nastase and other outstanding athletes have a more voluminous sense of time, a depth perception, within specific limits, of its grandness and promise.

1.21 ✍ THE STRIKING AWARENESS AND CONTROL of time achieved by great athletes hold analogies of importance to all of us. For time constitutes not only the medium of thought and feeling in general but also, to a significant extent, their very substance. To put it differently, our total ability to think and feel is directly proportional to the volume of thought or feeling we can hold in our minds within a given moment. Our two most basic intellective functions, the perception of likeness and the perception of difference, are best performed by trained minds which can, with apparent simultaneity, subsume two distinct phenomena and evaluate them in specific terms. Less skilled minds must rock the two ideas back and forth on a kind of seesaw until some analogy or distinction becomes clear to them. It would be imprecise to say that the trained mind thinks *faster* than the untrained mind, for some mental seesaws operate with frenetic speed; the good mind, we must rather put it, can within a given instant think *more*. In more

complex formulations, the advantages of this simultaneous awareness increase exponentially. The average philosophy professor, for
example, can summarize and expound upon, one by one, the hundreds of concepts and sequences in Plato's *Republic*. But ask him
how these components reflect upon each other, and he is likely to
take to the hills. The gifted student of philosophy, on the other
hand, is characteristically alert to these broad and implicit relationships. He realizes that it is in them, more than in any distinct and
explicit manifesto, that the meaning of the dialogue is contained.

1.22 ⚡ TITIAN's *Allegory of Prudence* (FRONTISPIECE)
is a three-leveled emblematic formulation of the proper attitude
toward time. From left to right, the three portraits (according to
Erwin Panofsky's convincing identification) are the painter himself, his son Orazio Vecelli and his relative and apprentice, Marco
Vecelli.* These faces at once represent old age, middle age and
youth, and, respectively, past, present and future. Beneath these
faces is a three-headed animal accepted in Renaissance iconography
as a mythological symbol of time. This nameless monster — wolf,
lion and dog in one — is early Egyptian in origin and occurs in the
first extant form as a companion of the sun god, Serapis. Its significance is glossed by the Roman scholar Macrobius as follows:

> The lion's head . . . denotes the present, the condition of which,
> between the past and the future, is strong and fervent by virtue of
> present action; the past is designated by the wolf's head because the
> memory of things that belong to the past is devoured and carried
> away; and the image of the dog, trying to please, signifies the out-
> come of the future, of which hope, though uncertain, always gives
> us a pleasing picture.†

Above the human heads is a motto which gives both coherence and
moral direction to the painting as a whole:

---

* Panofsky, *Meaning in the Visual Arts* (New York: Doubleday, 1957), pp.
146–168.
† Ibid., p. 153 (Panofsky's translation).

EX PRAETERITO	PRAESENS PRUDENTER AGIT	NI FUTURA ACTIONE DETURPET
"[Learning] from the past,	the present acts prudently,	lest it ruin future action."

The painting is a classic rendering of one of the dominant Renaissance precepts of right action. It was characteristic of the Renaissance to seek truth in "time" (history and direct experience) rather than in the divine or human "authorities" which had been so important to the Middle Ages. It was also typical of the Renaissance to elevate prudence (earthly *savoir-faire*) to a very high position among the virtues. And such practical wisdom was often, as here, expressed in mysterious pagan imagery.

The painting also has autobiographical significance.* Panofsky's hypothesis is that Titian, then nearly ninety, intended it to commemorate the prosperous completion of his own career and the continuity of his art in younger hands. In this sense the younger faces can be seen not only as individuals but also as aspects of a communal identity in art which stretches across the generations.

With regard to both levels of meaning, it should be noted that the three dimensions of time are seen as part of a single coherent being and suggest the notion of time as a continuum. However, only the face of present time looks directly out of the painting at the viewer. Light is projected from the right, the future: an apparent paradox, for the motto tells us to learn from the past. But the paradox disappears when we remember that objects are clearly seen only by the light they reflect, while when we look directly into a light source, just as when we look into the future, we see only outlines.

1.23 ✍ OUR METAPHORICAL AWARENESS OF TIME is complicated by the fact that our lives seem to extend backward against its grain. We naturally associate the past — the old — with our youth, and the young future with our old age. Thus we have trouble integrating psychological identity with the encompassing process of nature and history.

---

* Ibid., pp. 164–168.

1.24   PERSPECTIVE OPERATES IN TIME AS WELL as space. Long periods, like the years when we wore braces on our teeth, seem short to us when we are thirty-five; but last month's two-week vacation still has length and body in our memories. The year before us and the year just past seem immense and multileveled, like two deep valleys on either side of the ridge we occupy; the years beyond on either side, like farther valleys, seem progressively shallower and less detailed. To some extent this alienation from the continuum is inevitable, both physically and psychologically. But just as certainly, the degree of isolation from past and future varies from individual to individual; and those people who can, relatively speaking, control and inhabit their own past and future, have a particular dignity. It can be said, for example, that self-respect is impossible without respect for one's own past, and that coherent action in the present is impossible unless it is based on a vision that extends with some specificity into the future. How is such dignity won? Poetic as such an effort may seem, the past and the future cannot be sought and won as things in themselves. As part of a continuum, they have in essence no qualitative distinction from each other at all. Paradoxically, they can be approached effectively only when we come to terms, as openly and intimately as possible, with the one dimension of time which can be studied and questioned directly, the present. One may know the whole of a continuum from one segment of its arc. Indeed, people who seem to know the past and the future well have a habit of conceiving of them as forms of present time.

1.25   CONVERSELY, WE CANNOT COME TO TERMS with·the present until we learn to think of it (1) as part of the distant future (as it once was), and (2) as part of the distant past (as it will someday be). We must learn to do this not just with "present" time as an abstract entity, but with the present in combination with its indivisible spatial coordinates — the houses and rooms we sit in, our loved ones as they now appear, the state of our work, of our own body, of our very spirit. In the same way that we photograph major events, or that we seek, with anticipatory nostalgia, to encapsulate in our minds the elusive essence of a child's beauty, we must appreciate and memorialize every present state of mind as a unique wholeness, a transitory and irreproducible inter-play of force and substance. To do this is not only to value the present but to grow beyond it; for we are not only savoring and understanding present time more fully, but also surveying it, as if from hypothetical mirrors placed in past and future, in its perspec-tive in the continuum. Through this vision we may take an early step in the philosophical — indeed almost mystical — process of es-caping from the confines of momentary being; we may transcend the anxieties, prejudices, heaped-up assumptions and monstrous oversights which might otherwise dominate present time.

1.26 ✍ WHAT IS IDENTITY IN TIME? FOR A moment, imagine that you are an average middle-class drudge, whose life swings, from day to day, on a regular pendulum between obligatory work and listless recreation. Draw a spatial picture of yourself, and you will see a distinct being, independent, autono-mous, and separated from encompassing reality by several square feet of skin. But draw, if you can, a *temporal* picture of yourself, and you will see a veritable blob, shaped mainly by external pres-sures and, where no such pressures exist, swelling out amoebically into the void. Your temporal formlessness, in other words, belies your spatial coherence. Only by asserting yourself in time can you achieve functional identity and become in fact what you seem to be in the mirror. And such an assertion is impossible without a plan of personal development which forcefully projects your character into the future.

1.27 ✍ YOUNG PEOPLE ERR THROUGH IGNORANCE; but older people err through oblivion to dramatic but simple truths, learned and forgotten a hundred times. The ignorance of the young has the inviting vacancy of the outdoors; but the oblivion of the old is a noxious void behind a sneer of wisdom.

1.28 ✍ ALL GREAT EXPERIENCE HAS A GUARDED entrance and a windowless façade.

1.29 ⚘ TRUTH IS RHYTHMICAL: IF IT IMPLIES
stasis, it is platitude. Truth is syncopated: if it supplies all the
terms, there is one term too many. Truth is barbed: if it comforts,
it lies. Truth is an armed dancer.

1.30 ⚘ TO FRANCESCA FARIDANY, ON HER BAPTISM

Francesca, Nana's hope and Edward's treasure,
We multitude of shapes and smoke and mirth,
With manners strange to you in form and measure,
Are met to frame the season of your birth.

Between the closeness that protects your eyes
And the dry habit that imprisons ours
There is a countryside of mysteries,
A distance traced in lanes and dizzy moors.

Inland we labor with a solemn skill
To wrestle harvests from aridity;
You, far beyond our weary clamor, still
Can hear the muted laughter of the sea,

But cannot stay, no matter how you love
The gentle waves or their unmeasured grace,
For time, that brought you happy to the cove,
Must bring you yearning to this dusty place.

Nor can I offer prayer or prophecy
But that you keep and carry and hold dear
A stolen dram of laughter from the sea
To mock and moisten all the dryness here.

II ⚘ BONDAGE
IN TIME ⚘⚘⚘

II.1 ⚘ OUR NOTION OF FREEDOM IS ETCHED IN space. At pains to define liberty, that most resolute of indefinables, our minds fall back on spatial images: on birds, sailboats and mountains; the untethered balloon, the blue sky, the nude figure. Associations like these, all suggesting the exercise of will in absence of restraints, dominate our attitude toward freedom, extending beyond imagination into language, morality and politics. Yet experience persistently confutes this image and the assumptions which inhere in it. For the cosmos extends into four dimensions, not three; its laws are not exclusively spatial, but are rather the laws of space-time. These laws, which operate as much within us as outside of us, are all but impervious to three-dimensional images and concepts, which can unlock only a fraction of their structure and their force. When we ignore the temporal dimension, our conclusions about experience, though at a given moment they may seem full of insight, tend to fade and scatter like smoke; and we are left wondering whether it is the world around us, or we ourselves, that have so irreparably changed. To be effective, our understanding must comprehend the four-dimensionality of experience; our freedom, which is inseparable from understanding, must be freedom in time as well as freedom in space.

But that is easier said than done. The space-time continuum, an ocean of mobile interrelationships, is of maddening volume and variety. Faced with the problem of free choice in this kaleidoscope of kaleidoscopes, the mind is terrified if not benumbed. Characteristically, either conscious of our own weakness or in an automatic impulse of self-defense, we revert to such two- and three-dimensional models of reality as I have just mentioned. And by virtue of this surrender to the fourth dimension we become, after a fashion, hostages to it, locked in time in the same way that other prisoners are locked in space.

II.2   WHAT DO I MEAN BY "LOCKED IN TIME"? I mean, first of all, that we characteristically view mobile phenomena in immobile terms. We see processes like love and education as established circumstances rather than as complex temporal organisms whose lives depend on regular nourishment and renewal. Conversely, we tend to accept our own fear, weakness and ignorance as chronic disabilities rather than facing them, as we should, with the awareness that they are temporary and surmountable. Like still cameras, our minds consistently convert motion into stasis. In our language about time we resort to rocklike absolutisms — *creation, completion, means, end, permanence, annihilation* — terms whose static and extreme implications make them poor approximations of history and experience. We strike weak postures before time, adhering to concepts whose very pretensions to stability make them vulnerable to confusing change. We have little use at all for that most subtle and suggestive of words, *renewal,* and we have no word at all for the opposite of renewal, that composite of change and challenge which makes renewal necessary. Founded on such limited and ineffectual supports, our attitudes toward time are like sand castles, in constant need of rebuilding or propping up.

II.3   WE ARE INSENSITIVE TO NATURAL AND historical cycles, and hence we are always being taken by surprise. We concern ourselves with superficialities, with the skin of time rather than its heart. An old tree falls, a landmark is torn down, a career takes a sudden leap or drop, a friend dies of a heart attack; and we view these events as great acts of time, rather than (more accurately) the surface results of processes which continue in all things. Intent on such relative trivia, we not only miss the reality of time but also fall desperately behind it. Listening for the chimes, we fail to hear the clock — the soft pulse of growth and decay, the repeatedly whispered assents and refusals, the unassertive but coherent processes which carry the real burden of change. We view history with bewilderment and current development with comical surprise. Faced with the carcasses of events rather than events themselves, we strive in vain to bring about or prevent that which in effect has already happened.

II.4 ✍ WE STARVE, NEGLECT, INSULT AND variously abuse our memories, treating them more like filing cabinets, to store and regurgitate the minor data we need from day to day, than like living and creative elements of identity. We blink dumbly at the other powers of memory — its haunting retentiveness, its impish selectivity, its ability to barrage us with unnecessary information or to desert us completely in hours of need, its profound intercourse with the unconscious — without trying to comprehend or benefit from these functions. This uneasy relationship with a rich and voluminous intellectual resource is a sign of our distance from ourselves, and more particularly of our failure to recognize our own extensions in time. Our memories take their revenge for this lack of respect and cultivation with slowdowns, walkouts, bitter satires and outrageous midnight rallies.

II.5 ✍ MORE GENERALLY, OUR AWARENESS IS SO isolated in present time — and only a part of the present for that matter — that we do not grant to the past and the future the sort of attention they deserve. We usually fail to understand that the present achieves full reality only when seen by those who retain the perspectives of past and future, that indeed no aspect of time is really available to us except in terms of the continuum. Psychologically, moreover, we are alienated from our past and future selves, or rather, from our past and future extensions of self. We imagine ourselves, in many important ways, to be magically distinct from our own past; and we frequently disregard our own almost inescapable continuity into the future. Cut off both externally and internally from the native flow of experience, we are provincials in time, and show our lack of sophistication with any number of chronological *faux pas*.

II.6 ⬧ ALTHOUGH OUR METHODS OF KEEPING time are highly advanced, our methods of reckoning time are archaic, illogical and complex. The minutes in an hour, the hours in a day, and the days in a week are all counted according to different number systems, none of which fully utilizes the advantages of decimal notation. This sin against reason is compounded by the needlessly irregular lengths of our months. Measured time, which should possess the clarity and symmetry of metric space, is instead a jumble of dissimilar and irregular forms. Our own universally-accepted method blinds us to the natural coherence of time, turning the simplest calculations into difficult and painful problems.

II.7 ⬧ WE COMMONLY CONCEIVE OF TIME AS something external to ourselves. Modern physics has established time and space as parts of the same continuum and thus by implication integrated time into the heart of all things perceived; but modern language, common sense and humanistic inquiry lag far behind. We still speak and think in clichés which suggest that time is outside of us, something which "passes," something we can "spend," "serve" or "kill"; something which, though admittedly a part of the natural order, runs a course of its own. While natural science has attained a temporal understanding which is not only realistic but strangely beautiful and evocative, our own more general awareness of time has changed little since the days when Galileo was hauled before the Inquisition. Our world of time is as flat and exclusive as some medieval map.

II.8 ⬧ PARTLY AS A RESULT OF THIS, AND PARTLY to assuage our sense of temporal impotence, we vilify time, characterizing it as an adversary, a destroyer of things (*tempus edax rerum*), calling on it to fly or to stop, asserting our own identities in contradistinction to and in spite of it. We isolate time from the web of experience and regularly hang it in effigy, while seeking to portray ourselves, as "conquerors" of time, in effigies of granite or brass. In this we mock not time but ourselves, grimly distorting our sense of identity and our notion of the human spirit. For time is our medium both in our impermanence and in our permanence; and saying that someone is destroyed by time is as nonsensical as saying that someone is drowned by air.

II.9 ✍ FINALLY, THOUGH WE ARE MUCH MORE extensive and powerful in time than we are in the other three dimensions, our days and our lives are pathetically shortened by miscellaneous abuses and confusions of time. We are novices at the art of making plans and have trouble remembering the plans we have made. We ignore the time that is open to us. We diminish ourselves by wishing time to pass. We are, for the most part, incapable of real concentration. Our days are broken by distraction, scrambled up into muddles of chores, errands, impulses, evasions, interruptions and delays, besotted with routine. We characteristically fail to see the ways in which a given period can be expanded, deepened and slowed by the exercise of will and awareness. Deprived of this power and isolated from continuity, we often feel small, momentary, almost transparent, like paper-thin façades of being.

II.10 ✍ TO WHAT EXTENT IS IT POSSIBLE TO liberate ourselves in time? To the extent that we accept four-dimensional reality as the necessary context of free will. We may explore this potential freedom in the following ways:

· Use metaphor to visualize, as fully and variously as possible, time as a physical dimension.
· Become more acquainted with our own extensions in time, our past and future selves.
· Simplify calculations, become alert to the coherence between the longer and shorter periods of time.
· Increase our general awareness of the function of time in nature and in history.

- Revive and cultivate our memory.
- Reconcile ourselves with the innerness of time, ending the general state of war in which we have seen time as passing us, eroding us, alien to us.
- Study the travesties and beauties of time, and the human vices and virtues that most pertain to it.
- Learn the art of planning and, more generally, the art of extending will through time.

II.11 ✍ BACON SAYS THAT TO CONQUER NATURE, we must first obey it; but man, who has humbled himself toward space and matter, is still proud toward time.

II.12 ✍ ACCORDING TO ARISTOTLE (*Physics*, 220a), time is a dimension of motion. Such a definition, encouraging the inference that time is extrinsic to elemental matter, is still common in nonscientific thought on the subject. But modern physics has qualified Aristotle's definition in important ways. Special relativity has established time as a dimension of all things, whether they seem to us to be "moving" or not. Quantum mechanics has shown that on the subatomic level matter itself has, to some extent, wave nature and therefore motion. Thus time is not only a dimension of motion but also an ingredient of matter. Time is not an influence affecting things and relationships, but rather an essential element of things and relationships. The cosmos is not so much a thing in motion as a thing *of* motion, a complex interplay of energies and paces.

My aim is to project a theory of this sort into the realm of human awareness and will.

II.13 ✍ TO ILLUSTRATE HIS RESPECT FOR traditional English building techniques, a friend told me a story about a building contractor who was commissioned to tear down an old English barn. Common practice in these cases is apparently to hitch one's bulldozer to the uphill corner post and pull it out diagonally until the structure collapses. This man secured his chain to the post in question, mounted his machine, and began tugging away, without any noticeable results. He gritted his teeth and opened up the throttle until finally, with an awful wrenching and dragging noise, the bulldozer began to move. The contractor looked back to see the whole barn following him up the hill in one piece.

We have all heard stories of this kind; in general they are used to accord nobility to those products of human art and effort which "resist the ravages of time." But perhaps the opposite is true. We do not say, for example, that the ancient builders of this barn kept their edges true, their angles square and their boards flush *in order to resist the ravages of space*. Rather, they did these things in compliance with the laws of the three dimensions; and this compliance, it seems, brought them into accord with the fourth dimension, time. More generally, it can be argued that all things which endure do so by achieving harmony with the order of the four dimensions. Conversely, things built in defiance of this order, like the enormous Gothic cathedral piled up by the pretentious citizens of Beauvais, fall and crumble.

II.14 ✍ TIME'S MOST OBVIOUS DIMENSION IS linear, from past through present to future; but other necessary attributes of time complicate our understanding of it and make a one-dimensional interpretation, at least on the psychological level, all but impossible. In the first place, time is, like space, measured and defined only by what interrupts it. The phenomena which interrupt time are generally complex, containing two or more elements which exist *contemporaneously*. Contemporaneity may be charted as a line (Time₁) extending at right angles *across* the original time line (Time₂) and resulting in a two-dimensional image:

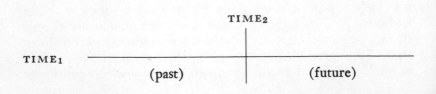

Moreover, we typically see phenomena not as flat but rather as voluminous and indeed massive; there is no more accurate image than this for the way in which important past or future events tend in our minds to overshadow or block out the smaller events around them, or the way in which present experience can blind us to past and future. Our composite perception of time is thus a kind of anti-space, a mental geography similar in laws and proportions to the corporeal world.

II.15 ⚸ TRAVELING TOWARD THE HIGH mountains, we can distinctly see the snow-peaks from a distance; but as we come closer they often disappear behind the convexity of the land — the lower but nearer hills. Once we are over the pass, these hills vanish completely and permanently; and looking back we see only the naked mass of the peaks themselves. It is much the same way with events. As important happenings approach, we tend to become so tied up in their preliminaries — the mailing of invitations or the packing of belongings, the lost roadmaps, the forgotten items, the apparently gratuitous squabbles — that the major events themselves are occluded and can no longer be seen in perspective. Yet once the central phenomenon is past, these petty and nervous preliminaries are the first things we forget. Together with our fears, our desires and our predictions, they are lost among the foot-hills of time; and looking back we see one great and coherent form, one deceptively simple shape of experience. We might be grateful for this oblivion, except for the fact that through it we are continually blinded to process, stripped of our sense of the real volume of time and isolated in the often quite unredeeming present. Without a broader temporal awareness we are as tiny on the face of our own lives as wayfarers on the Khyber Pass.

II.16 ⚸ IN OUR MINDS THE PAST, ON ONE SIDE, and the future, on another, tend to assume an immobile and two-dimensional composition, while the experience of the present is three-dimensional and enveloping. Before an event, we look toward its future face: an image strong in form, weak in detail, colored brightly by will and emotion – a kind of Impressionist painting of time. Afterward we look back on its past face: a resolution often uncertain in form but strong in detail – a news photo on the screen of memory. While we are in the midst of an event, surrounded by it, we usually lose all sense of shape and rather perceive multi-plicity, variety, unintegrated experience. Our minds do strange things with this tripartite phenomenology. Once an event is past, we almost automatically forget its old future face – as though our past will and expectation were of no significance at all, as though merely having experienced a phenomenon had made us wiser about it in every way than we were before it occurred. We forget about what we feared it to be, what we desired it to be; and in so doing we generally lose touch with the ways in which *we made it what it was*. Similarly we tend to lose touch with its body, its present-ness – the upsetting and/or exhilarating experience of being in the midst of it. We confidently accept the analysis of memory, our resident historian (who is, incidentally, as subject to emotion and prejudice as any other aspect of our awareness), rather than using the totality of the event as a means of understanding the temporal nature of experience and our active role in creating it.

II.17 ✑ TEMPORAL PATTERN, THOUGH AS pronounced and as natural as spatial pattern, is a great deal more difficult to recognize. For while spatial pattern is simultaneously before us, temporal pattern presents us with only one part or aspect at a time. Any of these aspects is easy to confuse with an aspect of another pattern or with mere chance; especially at the beginning of things, when there is no certainty that a pattern has been developing at all. Take, for example, the onset of an illness, the beginning of anger or anxiety, the roots of disaffection. More-over, the crisis of an experience, which is in a sense the center of temporal pattern, tends to obscure the earlier phases (which in our relief or exhaustion we often forget), making these prelimi-naries harder to recognize when they occur again. Thus, while temporal patterns are as intimate to us as our own heartbeats, and equally prevalent in social and political intercourse, we feel ill at ease with them, sensing them, if at all, as an almost ghostly under-tone of experience, a persistent but indefinable *déjà vu*.

II.18 ✒ PARADOX IS THE LANGUAGE OF unconsidered time, the gauge of our inability to keep touch with process. The ecstasy vanishes in dullness; the child is suddenly an adult; the friendship of convenience dissolves in a puff of annoyance. We read a single obituary and the world, up to now a merry club of friends, becomes as empty as a condemned tenement. These surprises afflict us not because of any chronic defect of vision, but rather because we tend to be consumed by, even prostituted to, the miscellaneous concerns of the present, unwilling to carry the frightening sweep of the past and future along with us through daily life.

II.19 ✒ LOVERS WHO PLOD MECHANICALLY through a series of unsuccessful relationships are good examples of the failure to understand the dimensionality of time. At the beginning of each affair or marriage they forget what sickened them about the last; in the middle they forget what brought them into it; and at the end they fail to perceive the causal relationship between their initial desire, their half-hearted participation and their inevitable failure. Like adding machines they return faithfully to zero after each sum and are ready for the next transaction. People who chronically fail to complete projects are subject to similarly frustrating revolutions of will. This is not to say that an awareness of our emotional cyclicality will be a sure cure for our characteristic problems. But it is certainly a first step — in fact the only first step. Unconscious enslavement is enslavement doubled.

II.20 ✒ WHAT I PROPOSE IS A HABIT OF LOOKING not only at but *through* past and future events and of endowing present time with its past and future dimensions.

Think of some past event like your high school graduation. We generally look at such events as flat things hung on the wall of the past. This time try to reassemble your thoughts leading up to the event, your feelings while it was in progress. Your sense of what actually happened is likely to change; the event is likely to take form and stand out against the background of the past.

You have just spent a day that started with great cheer and resolve but unaccountably diminished into an emptiness of muddle and distraction. Review the day's events and emotions in order.

You have a day to spare and wish to use it well. You see yourself in a kind of compartment of time whose immediate walls are last night's and tonight's sleep. Look beyond these walls and back at the present from imaginary mirrors placed in the past and the future. Think of the choices and events which brought you where you are; think of what you once wished or expected to have achieved by this point. Imagine what you will think of this period some time in the future. Will you think or do anything today that is worthy of future memory?

Try to make the present memorable; or, failing this, review daily what is important about the present period in your life. In so doing you will enrich time.

II.21 ✒ WE CANNOT PROJECT SPACE-TIME INTO psychological experience without profound changes in perception and comprehension. By fiat of four-dimensionality, "what" becomes "what/when," "who" becomes "who/when," "you" and "I" and everything undergo similar transformations. A challenging idea, implying that identities and relationships are always in motion; that attempts to codify them in static, absolute terms are at very best relative and approximate. To some observers this might suggest absolute relativism, loss of identity, chaos. But this extreme hypothesis seems to be true neither in science nor in human affairs. Things may change; but they change at characteristic rates and in characteristic ways, recognizable and natural. We search for character, value, truth, not so much like pilgrims seeking a marble shrine, as like listeners perceiving, in different musical instruments at different times, recurring themes and rhythms. Thus a kind of stability — perhaps the only real stability — exists in space-time, and our ability to recognize this mobile truth bears the same proportion to normal common sense as physics bears to solid geometry.

II.22 ✒ WHEN WE SPEAK OF THE RELATIVITY OF time, we are generally referring to modern physics, where time is seen as relative to motion. Yet time is relative, and confusingly so, in much more immediate ways. The same physical unit of time may seem long or short to us, depending on our mood or activity. Different beings seem to live according to different time scales; and in the animal world the housefly, with its innumerable little alarms and escapades, may experience as much in a day as a Galapagan tortoise does in a decade. Volunteers, immured for weeks in caves without reference to clocks, note strange distortions in their sense of time and their physiological rhythms. Without the normal cosmic and social props, their bodies seek new rhythms, or perhaps begin to lose rhythm and coherence altogether.

We go to sleep, and time speeds by us like starlight, whisking us hours closer to the grave. Yet sleep rejuvenates; these lost hours slow down aging and keep us young; time running fast means that Time will run slow.

II.23 ✍ OUR SENSE OF THE SLOWNESS OR SPEEDINESS of time often depends on the size of the time-frame we happen to be considering. It is possible, for example, for us to be simultaneously amazed at the slowness of minutes and the speediness of years. Oddly enough, this pathetic double amazement bespeaks a single cause: our inability to make proper use of the present. For although minutes spent in boredom or anxiety pass slowly, they nonetheless add up to years which are void of memory.

II.24 ✍ IF THE WORDS "TO HAVE" AND "TO KNOW" are taken in their deepest sense, then there is nothing in the world that we may truly have or know. In most of our experiences — personal, professional, political, esthetic — we stand at the periphery, conversant with detail but unsure about structure, basis, context; unsure even about the nature of the emotions that the experience evokes in us. What we understand best, we understand by renewal — by looking at the same thing again and again in different ways, looking at it internally and externally, walking around it, turning it in our hands, participating in it until some strange abstract spirit of its being rises from the complexity of effort and detail. And what we have best, we have by renewal — by chronic challenges never refused, by danger of loss, by repeated cherishings, and by love remembered.

II.25 ✍ JUST AS SPATIAL FREEDOM IS IMPOSSIBLE without a sense of context and limit, freedom in space-time is impossible without a sense of the larger cycles of experience which encompass and define our lives. Pain, anxiety and boredom, though common to all of us, are diminished by our awareness of the broader setting in which they develop and subside. Hard work, originally undertaken through necessity or in order to achieve a goal, crystallizes into pleasure as we grow in skill; and we return to it daily less as an isolated challenge than as a kind of temporal home, a welcome and familiar channel of identity. Recreation itself gains richness to the extent that we see something of our own in it, something we have had before and will have again. Paradoxically, the unique value of any experience is lost unless we appreciate its repetitive nature and mark it as a recurring voice in the music of time.

II.26 ✍ IN GENERAL WE ARE SURPRISED BY EVENTS not so much because they refute our expectations as because we have no coherent expectations at all. We look at the future as at a kind of mirror, which faithfully reproduces the concerns of the present but glassily denies their projection into the continuum.

II.27 ✍ ANYWHERE WE GO, WE CAN, WITH GREAT freedom and relatively small chance of disagreement, insult the times we live in. But we cannot criticize the place where we happen to be, even if it is our own native town, without the risk of giving serious offense. The latter circumstance is easily understandable, for people tend to identify with their own locale and to feel responsible for it; the former, however, implies an evasion of responsibility as pernicious as it is epidemic. For just as there is no qualitative distinction between space and time, there is no moral justification for viewing one, and not the other, as an extension of our own will. This disavowal of reality springs, I believe, from a deep psychological malaise, a chronic sense of impotence which, unable to vilify its own corporeal immediacy, makes the subtlest of the four dimensions its traditional scapegoat. Using a variety of verbal postures and vulgar traditions, we feel that we can insult and diminish *when* we are without realizing that in doing so we also insult and diminish *what* we are. And in doing so we isolate ourselves, not only from our comprehensive reality but also from its implicit sources of freedom. Turning our backs on time, we turn our faces to the wall.

II.28 ✍ GENERALIZING ABOUT AN EVENT WHILE that event is in the process of occurring is like scanning the horizon from a hole. Yet we seldom generalize about events at any other time.

II.29 ✍ I OWN AN OMEGA WRISTWATCH WHICH I bought nine years ago at Heathrow Airport and which has since then produced for me, with reasonable fidelity to nature, about 700 million ticks and tocks. Almost every day, winding it, I am reminded that another day has run out, that I am one day farther down the line. Sometimes I glance too at the hand and wrist beneath the watch, which, with their growing assortment of scars, lines and shadows, are also accurate time-keepers, suggesting not daily minutiae but rather my definite position between the entrance and exit of life. Locating myself in the larger picture, I momentarily leave the thicket of daily concerns and sense a more urgent pulse (days ticking like seconds, ages passing like hours) which animates my life. If some eccentric had his watch dismantled and a tiny death's head etched upon the face, I would understand and sympathize.

II.30 ⚹ THE ACCEPTANCE OF SPACE-TIME SUGGESTS a rapprochement between those two appalling terms, *infinity* and *eternity*. One way of integrating these two terms in a mental construct of space-time is the hypothesis that any point where/when an observer stands constitutes the outer limit of the space-time cosmos, that from this point the observer may look backward through limitless history but forward only into the void. In terms of this hypothesis, the observer sits in space-time as though facing backward in the taut concavity of a wind-stretched sail.

III ✎ ✎ ✎ PAST, PRESENT AND FUTURE ✎ ✎ ✎

III.1 ✎   **TIME IS ONE, BUT IN OUR MINDS IT IS** several. Considering, for a moment, time's three dimensions as mental vessels, we store our accidents in the past, our worries and desires in the present; and we preserve the future as a virginal receptacle for hope and will. We think, for example, of our next trip abroad as a majestic exploration concocted exclusively of quaint landscapes, delightful meetings, elegant meals, artistic wonderment and quiet epiphanies in sunlit outdoor cafes. The future trip is somehow purged of the characteristics which all but identified our earlier trips: the anxiety about being late, the lack of comfortable chairs and private space, the enslavement to money changers, the backbreaking marriage to our portable belongings, the stomach aches, the agonies of language, the inevitable family fights. For most of us, it is these latter things, more than the former, which give travel its palpable texture in time and which, paradoxically, provide us with the deep and relieving sense of change travel gives. We do not forget the pains of travel; they are stitched inextricably into the quilt of tatters we call the past. But we chronically fail to project them into the future, to see that such miscellanies of accident and circumstance will mold the future as they have molded the past, and to understand that only painful and vigorous attention will achieve any basic alteration in the quality of time.

III.2 ✎   **ONE OF THE MOST MYSTERIOUS OPERATIONS** of time is the way in which things silently divorce themselves from us and slip into the past. We are like people climbing out of an immensely deep valley on a trail which only occasionally allows us glimpses of the geography below or the heights above. We turn to see, distant and small beneath us, places which only recently have constituted our total environments; we glance far down at our own beginnings as things dear but inexorably removed from us. Other people walk with us, so close and for so long that they form a part of our identity. When they leave us at last, we see them for the first time as separate beings, suddenly clear and whole, yet hopelessly distinct and diminishing. Only those of us who habitually and affectionately consult the past, who see the present as the birth of the past and appreciate it as the freshness of a new vintage, can hope to mitigate the appalling sadness of these views.

III.3   IN THE SAME WAY THAT OUR EYES HAVE blind spots in space, our minds have blind spots in time; areas of time which we habitually or congenitally ignore. My own blind spot is the recent past, the events of yesterday or last week. I experience things quite fully in the present; but then they submerge, not to reappear until they are images on the flat wall of the past. Why is this so? Is there something uncomfortable, raw, undigested, embarrassing about the jumble of experience just behind me? Is it ignored because it is simply too chaotic to make sense? Look at the past day, the past hour: their interruptions, frivolities, compromises, false starts. We may well have good reason to overlook the immediate past, for the immediate past holds the uncensored truth of the present.

III.4   FROM HIS EXILE AT SAN CASCIANO, Machiavelli wrote a friend that he spent much time reading the works of ancient writers, adding curiously that he asked them questions which they "answered." What he probably meant was that, like Machiavelli himself, the ancients wrote subtly, that they raised questions in the reader's mind and encouraged him to seek out the answers to these questions between the lines, in the stylistic and structural implications of their work. Good historians treat the past in general this way, asking it questions rather than contenting themselves with its overt and specific messages. And intelligent individuals treat their memories in the same way, realizing that their past is no more finished or dead than their ability to understand it.

III.5 🖎 THE FRENCH USE THE TERM "ESPRIT DE *l'escalier*" ("wit of the stairway") to describe the brilliant comments that occur to us just after we have left the party or meeting where they would have been appropriate. The killing response to an unprovoked insult, the *quietus* for an aggressive bore, the naughty paradox that would have made you shine, are as useless now as tickets to last night's show. So much is wit the child of time. Still, it is not just our own slowness that makes us think of things too late. Something in the social experience itself, some fear of self-expression or some awareness of wit's proximity to the utterly absurd, deadens our minds and stops our tongues. Besides, the witty remark, whether it denudes hypocrisy or subverts language, is always a miniature revolution, a gesture of reform. The witticism makes its creator, at least momentarily, an enemy of established society; and thus wit is as much a child of courage as it is of time.

III.6 🖎 IT IS ODD THAT WHILE PHYSICAL PAIN vanishes completely, and profound grief is finally softened and healed, the regret of our own misdeeds stays fresh as a daisy. And with me it is not even the major sins that are most painful, but rather the petty misdemeanors, which hover at the curtains of memory like misshapen gnomes, always ready to prance out onto the stage. Perhaps I have already done penance for the real sins; perhaps no reasonably healthy person can injure others without suffering the injury himself. The misdemeanors, on the other hand, which really injure no one else, are pure checks to the ego; they evoke shame, not guilt.

Even more upsetting for me than this, though, is the foggy and diffuse presence in memory of a million things left undone. The pain of having erred palpably or having deserved derision is certainly sharper; it is an acid that the past, like a resentful stomach, serves up again and again. But the memory of things which (perhaps even through fear of erring) I did *not* do — of a desert of hesitations, evasions, refusals, anxieties and wasted hours — is less like pain than like imprisonment, isolation within the confines of my own weakness. Dante has a special place in upper hell for *"l'anime triste di coloro / Che visser sanza infamia e sanza lodo,"** the unhappy spirits of those who lived without blame and without praise. He implies that willed action, which always holds the risk of blame, is also the only way to salvation.

III.7 ⚞ IN THE LATE 1970S, U.S. SOCIETY WAS gripped by an epidemic desire to discover its "roots," and millions of people suddenly began to consult genealogies, etymologies and chronicles in efforts to uncover their family backgrounds. This movement, for all its gross faddishness, showed signs of having significant social and psychological causes. Perhaps people saw in "roots" a chance to reestablish a forgotten element of identity; and a society, grown fat and fatuous on the present, finally sensed the connection between its disregard for the past and its own haunted loneliness.

III.8 ⚞ ONE NEED ONLY TRY TO REMEMBER the dishes one ate for dinner on each night of the week past to realize that the things we desire as future and enjoy as present are not necessarily the things we value for all time. In this sense memory sits like an incorruptible judge, oblivious to the minor pains and pleasures of the past even as we unreasonably overvalue identical pains and pleasures in the present and future.

---

* *Inferno*, canto 3.

III.9 🦢 YESTERDAY WAS MY SON ANTHONY'S
third birthday, and we hosted a party in the sunny courtyard by
our front door in Carmel Valley. Our neighbor Joe Lawrence ap-
peared bearing a ponderous yellow and pink cake; five of Anthony's friends came and frolicked in the late afternoon; adults
stopped by for drinks; my mother-in-law took care of little Edward Nicholas; Anthony's babysitter brought her husband and a
small rabbit. Amidst the six solemn faces topped with bright coni-
cal hats, the cake was cut and served with elaborate attention. As
with Anthony's two previous birthdays, I made a movie of the
event, titling it with a view of the place and date in the typewriter.
Long after everyone left, I went out to the courtyard to clean up.
In the sunset the empty yard was a gay shambles of balloons, ribbons, plates, hats, napkins, boxes and wrapping paper. The wreck-
age symbolized the experience of the whole event in time: how
things so painstakingly brought together — the six kids, all scrubbed
and tidied and ready on the hour, the cake, the presents, the hoped-
for good weather — hold with such temporally flimsy cement and
vanish forever, disengaging chaotically, like ribbons and spangles
in a windy courtyard. And yet, if the mixture has been right,
something like the soul of the experience remains, a memory as
elemental and incorruptible as a rainbow in the child's mind.

III.10 🦢 WE ALL SHARE A SENSE OF THE PRESENT;
but for some of us the present is a much more voluminous temporal body than for others. Some people cruise through time in
ocean liners; others labor along in wherries. Or, to mix the metaphor: let time be a stretch of white water which we set out to
conquer in separate canoes. The inexperienced boatsman alternates
between desperate responses to immediate necessities and recupera-
tive oblivion during easy sections. The experienced boatsman, on
the other hand, is always safely in channel because he has marked
the channel from up river. While his arms and torso respond to
immediate needs, his eyes look downstream. His mind has gauged
the mood of the river from the rapids he has already run; it notes
anything new or interesting for future reference. There is, simply
speaking, *more river* for him than for the inexperienced boatsman.
Thus the scope and volume of the present increase with the ex-

tent to which we have prepared for it and the extent to which we use it as preparation for things to come. And the largeness of our present is synonymous with our freedom in time.

III.11 ✍ HOW WILL WE, FIVE OR TEN OR TWENTY years hence, look back on present time? Most probably, with envy and regret. We will envy the younger self who could, relatively speaking, do so much; and we will regret that it did not do more. We will wonder why, given youth and health and broad reaches of time, we learned so little, loved so little, risked so little; how so much time could have drained so immemorially down the sink of routine and distraction. Yet these regrets, however specifically realistic they are, ignore the broader continuity, which dictates that the confines of a single moment can hold all the dimensions and potentialities of time, and that the crucial decisions and op- portunities are always before us, no less now than in the past, no less in the future than now.

III.12 ✍ MOST PEOPLE ARE TRAPPED IN THE present, unequivocally divorced from the two embracing dimen- sions of time. We are so harassed by circumstance or bewildered by events that, like climbers clinging to a single niche, we hold on to the present as last resort; or we are so full of nameless and faceless anxiety that the past vanishes outright and the future looks like a nauseous pit. We proclaim ourselves hedonists, de- nounce cause, effect, history and will as reactionary dogma, and live for the moment; or we become opportunists, dwelling like sociable outlaws in a world that offers nothing except danger and advantage. Whatever their abuse, most people live in the present like prisoners in some dark and narrow space. What happens in this space is never predictable; yet paradoxically it never seems strange or new. Our isolation in time is isolation from time; our devotion to the present deracinates and destroys the present.

III.13 🖎 EXCESSIVE SENSITIVITY TO THE DEMANDS of the present is the root of impotence. Pope Clement VII, regarded as one of the most vacillating figures in history, probably did not make a single decision which was not amply justified in his mind by emergent needs. Moreover, the present abhors precedents and is always trying to deny or obfuscate the existence of pattern. It claims to be a unique case, demanding special treatment and unusual indulgences. Failing its claim of preeminence, it falls back to one of total insignificance, that "this time it really won't matter"; and in desperation it may turn to "the hell with the rest of time; you and I are all that count." But there are no special cases in the normal course of things, no way in which the pattern of time can elevate or ignore an act of will. The person who characteristically obeys and serves the present becomes a kind of temporal microorganism and is, paradoxically, more likely than any other to follow fixed and slavish channels of behavior.

III.14 🖎 WE PAMPER THE PRESENT LIKE A SPOILED child, obeying its superficial demands but ignoring its real needs. Its familiar slogans (which include "Let's do it later," "Let's have a snack," "Time out!" "Ouch, that hurts," and "Not now — I'm fragile") can tyrannize us into oblivious days of distraction and impulsive chaos. Heeding these slogans, we are, paradoxically, unkind to the present, ignoring the opportunity to project it into the future, forgetting it as soon as it is past. As we would injure children by spoiling them, we injure time by being too attentive to its ephemera.

III.15 🖎 WE MOVE QUITE SWIFTLY THROUGH time; passing, in the course of a single hour, literally thousands of potentialities for perception, thought or action. Yet our time on earth is, relatively speaking, so immense (8,766 hours in a single year) that most often we seem to ourselves to be moving slowly, if at all. Because our perspective is so broad, we become insensitive to our real motion, like travelers in the middle of a voyage between the imperceptibly receding coastline of the land they have left and the imperceptibly heightening coastline of the land they are approaching. In fact, we tend to see the present as something almost motionless — more a state of being than a process of becoming. Like the hour- and minute-hands of a watch, our lives seem motionless, and we tend to float rather than swim in time. This illusion is in some ways healthy and even necessary. Going through life with the alacrity of a fly or a hummingbird, we would quickly destroy ourselves. On the other hand, by mistaking process for being and motion for stasis, we tend to fall out of touch with our reality in time — with the countless opportunities for enlightenment and will which are offered daily. Because we believe that one moment is more or less like the next, we lose touch with the essential urgency of the present, the fact that each passing moment is the one moment for the practice of freedom.

III.16 ⚹ AS WE GROW OLDER WE WISH MORE and more to be young again, to return to youth with the wisdom of age, or failing this, to get back to it any old way. We characteristically ignore a much more feasible kind of chronological magic — making present time slow its pace. For one must love life indeed, in all its miscellaneous fullness, in order to hanker that its smallnesses, its very dimples and indentations, be lengthened for one's pleasure. To wish such a thing is, in effect, to begin to do it; and to do it is to enlarge life immeasurably. One should think first of all of the present, not as a moving point or as a thin film through which one faces a parade of concerns, but rather as a kind of chamber, a voluminous dimension in which thoughts and actions and affections can develop undisturbed. One divides the day into large natural periods, so that the future, though secure, is never nagging or imperious. One seeks the larger projects, the designs which extend our care and effort through weeks and months. And one is constantly in touch with the past — not only with the distant events that form the basis of character, but also with the immediate past, yesterday's events, the morning's activities, the conversation just over. For we grip time as though with two hands; and loosening our hold on the past speeds and cheapens time's whole course.

III.17 ✍ TO THOSE OF US WHO SPEND ENTIRE days, if not lifetimes, concentrating on a series of brief and insignificant things, the present has barely any meaning at all; we become tiny timorous things, caught in the inch of space between the "in" box and the "out" box. While we may share the common illusions about a mobile present and a free future, we spend most of our lives housecleaning the past — maintaining commitments, counterbalancing errors, living up to expectations, mopping up our own postponements. In this sense, as in others, we shuffle backward into the future, unaware of our enslavement to time or of the simple freedom of new beginnings.

III.18 ✍ THE PRESENT GIVES US SIMULTANEOUSLY the illusion that it is exceptional and the illusion that it is eternal. Of course it is neither of these, but rather a recurrent and usually minor ambush of space and time where, like it or not, we must close ranks and fight. It teaches us nothing of importance, except that its grime and confusion are the fabric of living time; that no analysis of past time or projection of future time should ignore its prying demands and grudging allowances.

III.19 ✍ WE GET OUR SHARPEST TASTE OF THE present when we are frightened, harried or baffled; for then present time seems to lock us physically into itself and away from the continuum. This divorce from continuity is also, to all intents and purposes, a divorce from identity. I experienced something of this sort most vividly one afternoon in Spain during the fall of 1978. In the course of a hurried trip to America with a sick child, we drove to Malaga. A neighbor from La Herradura, who had offered to buy our car, came along with us to take possession; and as he was not well practiced in driving, I had to bring him some distance back along the road from Malaga to a point where he could begin his journey in lighter traffic. We stopped at an inn near the beach, and there, waiting for the cab to pick me up, we had a drink among a crowd of wild and jolly people down from the hills, who babbled to each other in Andalusian. The cab which took me back to Malaga was a ravaged Fiat whose suspension had long since worn away, leaving nothing but spongy upholstery between its passengers and the cratered road. We shuddered slowly through endless industrial suburbs. The air was hot, and ahead of us the setting sun was red with dust. The streets were full of men and women just off work. My mind was everywhere except within itself. I had packed up a year of Spanish life in three days. I was more anxious, and with more genuine cause, than I had ever been in my life. And in the midst of this mad rush I had somehow driven ten miles back away from the airport and the urgent future, as though life had lost all its normal reason and become a game of Monopoly in which I had made an unlucky toss. The usual sequence of cause and effect seemed interrupted if not overturned. The driver and I did not speak. Gaining the center of a suburb the cab entered a light brown cumulus, a sunny and indefinitely immense cloud of dust and smoke. I felt uniquely and undesirably cut off from time and space, from the sum of recallable characteristics that made me a person with a name.

III.20 ✒ THE PAST IS LIKE THE BODY OF TIME, the future like its soul. Our sense of the past is voluminous, corporeal, complex; but our sense of the future should hold innocently and simply, like a stellar spectrum, the full quality of our spirit and will.

III.21 ✒ THE FUTURE IS LIKE A FRIENDLY STRANGER, polite and patient, forever trying to get acquainted with us, forever being rebuffed. If we did simple exercises for thirty minutes a day, we would greatly improve our strength, health, beauty and life expectancy. If we studied for one hour a day, we could relatively soon learn languages, master wide knowledge and develop new professions. If we sensibly invested $1 a day, we would in thirty years control substantial wealth. If we did ourselves the almost absurdly simple honor of planning our free time, we would enlarge ourselves into a whole new dimension of freedom. Yet we often fail to do any of these things, so great is our contempt of the future, so massive our ignorance of ourselves. It would be for most of us a highly disagreeable experience to meet, in the flesh, our future selves. Not just for the visual shock of seeing our own spirits animating bent limbs, watery eyes and sagging jowls; but for the moral shock of meeting individuals whom we have daily and disgracefully wronged.

III.22 📧 THE BIRTH OF OUR SECOND CHILD IS ONE, maybe two weeks away. The coming event looms over us, the way a big wave looms over a little boat; and our days are dimmed by its shadow. The future can exert this force upon us, can totally suck the juice out of the present, turning it into something tense, dry, useless to memory. How can we enjoy or profit from such a transitional state? The practical answer is "Don't sit and wait; prepare." The subtler answer is that no period in life is more or less transitional than any other, had we only the power to understand each.

III.23 📧 CAN THE PAST AND PRESENT TEACH US anything about the future? In a mechanistically conceived universe, the future is locked up inside the past and present; they hold it with the graceful secrecy and diminutive perfection of a pomegranate holding its seeds. Yet we rebel against such a formulation, not only because it offends our sense of freedom but also because no prognosticator, however studious of past and present, has ever been able clearly to predict the future. But it is equally abhorrent to say that the past and present can tell us nothing about the future at all. A chaotic universe is as great an insult to freedom as a mechanistic one; and common sense avows that the past and present, correctly viewed, can offer much evidence about future probabilities. To put it differently, temporal experience is neither completely recurrent (in which case it would be wholly knowable) nor completely variable (in which case it would be wholly inscrutable). In effect, it is more like a piece of complex music, a Bach fugue heard for the first time. In one sense, we are excited and surprised by the novel disposition of tones and rhythms and by the uncanny variety of the treatment. In another sense, we realize that recurring ideas and cycles are what give the work its native character, and that the variations, however stunning, have significance only in terms of their relationship to these underlying themes. Conversely, the recurrent themes are realizable in their fullest sense only through the variations done upon them. The careful student of time is thus as sure that certain things will recur as he is sure that they will recur in dazzlingly new forms. He is sure that the future, like the past, will be full of accidents, but also that none of these accidents, however comic or tragic, will be chaotic or monstrous. And if he wishes to be truly prescient, he must exercise his knowledge not only on the outer world of events but also on the inner world of his own behavior and awareness. He must continually review his own strengths and weaknesses, his own loves, values, and goals. For the broadest window to the future lies in the continuity of the mind perceiving it and in the consistent vigor of the will entreating it. Only integrity knows the future.

III.24   WE ARE OFTEN PIQUED WHEN WE HEAR predictions, as though there were something vaguely immoral about them. And in a limited sense they are indeed immoral, constituting treasonous breaches of our habitual state of war with time. Yet prediction is natural to anyone who views time coherently. For if the future is a dimension of things, we cannot learn the nature of anything without also learning something about its future. We can predict, for example, that steep hillsides, denuded by fire, will erode in heavy rains, that paint applied to dirty surfaces will peel off, that unfenced vegetable gardens will be raided by rabbits or deer. More abstractly, we can predict that all fashionable items and ideas will shortly be unfashionable, that hyperbolical campaign promises will be believed and not kept, that extreme moral postures will soon evaporate or give way to their opposites. We can predict that spoiled children will grow bored and impatient, that neglected children will grow selfish and insecure, that love offered everyone will please no one, that love withheld from everyone will dry up and disappear. And we can predict that all these predictable events will come as utter surprises to the people involved.

III.25 ⚘ WE ALTERNATELY ENVY, PRAISE, despise and tease those unusual people who plan ahead, who keep precise calendars of when they will be where, seeing whom and doing what. Yet in all these posturings we tend to ignore a benefit of their behavior which is at once the simplest and the most spiritual. They can escape despair. They have cast tow-lines out to the future and can, when necessary, drag themselves through a becalmed or stormy present. And they have peopled the wilderness of things to come with images of themselves in action or relaxation or festive attire.

III.26 ⚘ AMONG THE MANY GOOD REASONS FOR making plans is the fact that the future can be enjoyed as fully as the present or the past. But most of what we enjoy, we enjoy specifically. A contemplated week in Paris, pleasant as a generalized concept, becomes much more pleasant when we know that it will include a visit to the Sainte-Chapelle, afternoons at the Louvre and Cluny, a splurge, a stroll on the Île St. Louis, an evening at the Opera preceded by cocktails at the cafe of the same name and followed by onion soup near the old site of Les Halles, a morning Metro-ride to the Jardin des Plantes or the Vincennes Zoo. In this way the projected days become a delightful union of the real and the ideal; and the future, huge yet as transparent and inconsequential as vacant sky, takes on dozens of meaningful shapes. People suspect that planning will shackle them; but, with moderation, this is almost never the case. If you make plans, you may always diverge from them — committing what is itself a pleasant act of freedom. If you do not make plans, you leave the future an empty field of chance, useless to the present, forfeit to your own unpredictable moods. You insult time, and it turns away from you a face that could have been full of solace. And you imply to yourself that the two other dimensions of time, past and present, mean less to you than they might or should.

III.27 ⚘ FOR MOST OF US THE FUTURE IS LIKE AN attic, unfinished raftered space, filled with deferred obligations and dismembered dreams. We take almost every opportunity to ignore, demean and otherwise abuse this dimension, and with good reason: it carries the upsetting challenge to laziness, fear and habit, the frightening impetus to self-knowledge, the painful and insistent voice of freedom.

III.28 ✍ HENRY JAMES'S *The Beast in the Jungle* is the story of a man who spends years awaiting a great and mysterious psychological event and finally realizes, far too late, that this experience had always been waiting, in all its intensity and completeness, on the simple exercise of his love and will. This great story is an allegory of the tyranny of the future. The future will do much for us, and we must do much for it. But one thing we must not do is imagine that it contains essential human qualities or unique opportunities which we now lack.

III.29 ✍ THE FUTURE IS LIKE THE DAYTIME moon, a diffident but faithful companion, so elegant as to be almost invisible, an inconspicuous marvel.

III.30 ✍ IN A STORY BY MAX BEERBOHM, A MINOR literary figure named Enoch Soames travels many years forward in time with the exclusive intention of finding his own name in a library index. He is crushed to discover that he has been forgotten, that his stylish endeavors have not won, from the future, the dignity of even a mention. Precisely so, in almost every case, our own futures will trail off into oblivion. Those few of us who are gifted, intensely industrious and very fortunate, would (should they travel a century forward in time) perhaps find their names in professional histories, followed by the usual parenthesized and hyphenated pair of dates and the economical description of some position or achievement. But the rest of us can hope at best (excepting local records) for affectionate memories among our families and friends, stories from our grandchildren beginning "My grandfather once . . . ," and then relatively speedy submersion into the bog of generations. We deal with this unpleasant fact in various ways. The majority, availing themselves of the classic preference for ignorance over terror, concentrate on not thinking about it at all. The doers among us hammer away at the face of time in hopes of establishing, in the end, a recognizable chink. But a few happy souls achieve, usually near the end of life, a seeming transparency of self, an awareness which dissolves the barrier between selfness and otherness and immerses itself in the continuity of life around them. An extreme example of this sense of the homogeneity of experience is Albert Einstein, who saw it not only in the world he would someday leave but in the encompassing breadth of time itself, and said that the past, the present and the future were all one.

IV IDENTITY, LOVE AND TIME

IV.1 TWO OF THE WORDS MOST DIFFICULT TO define satisfactorily are *self* and *other*. For, rightly understood, these two words relate crucially not only to the characteristics of given individuals, but also to the much larger question of what pertains fundamentally to the individual, what to the group or race. It can be argued forcefully, for example, that *individual* is itself a misleading term, that "individuals" are instead examples of a type, participants in a basically shared awareness. It has been urged further that neither the human race nor the biological kingdom limits our identity, so indivisible is life itself from its natural context.

One element of this question which interests me particularly here is the extent of identity in time. How much of our past and future do we acknowledge and actively treat as aspects of self, and how much do we reject or wholly ignore? A middle-aged man who once committed a violent crime disowns it as an act of youth, yet it haunts him like the ghost of an earlier identity. An ex-champion grown old and weak identifies affectionately with his past, yet feels he is an irredeemable exile from it. Young people, claimants to the future, look complacently at their pasts, still vivid and surrounding, as inalienable appurtenances. But to those others condemned fatally by age or disease, the past can seem flat as a mirror, fruitless and absurd. People so trapped and isolated in time seem disinherited from themselves, psychologically cut off from aspects of identity which might otherwise have given them wholeness.

IV.2 ✍ DYING BY SUICIDE AFTER A SERIES OF military disasters, Shakespeare's Antony urges Cleopatra to ignore the tragic present and think instead of the glorious past:

> The miserable change now at my end
> Lament nor sorrow at; but please your thoughts
> In feeding them with those my former fortunes
> Wherein I liv'd, the greatest prince o' th' world,
> The noblest . . .*

The force and beauty of this statement are compounded by the experience of the whole play, which strikes many interpreters as being less a tale of woe than an evocation of memorable joy and greatness, and less a testament to time's destructive powers than an uncommonly mature acceptance of its full pattern. Compare Antony's speech with thoughts *you* might have during your last moment alive, or even during a prolonged old age. The speech suggests an activity intrinsic to dignity and full awareness: the projection of self into dimensions other than the present.

This activity need be by no means limited to the proximity of death or the contemplation of the past alone. People of understanding constantly derive energy and support from past and future selves. They revisit their past selves — their notes, sketches, achievements, memories — with affection and curiosity, regularly renewing contact with expressions of personality which are at once strange and familiar. They love making plans and beginning projects, either confident that future selves will improve and complete what they have begun, or, if they are older, simply tasting the pleasure and solace of futurity. Realizing their coherence through time, they maintain touch with the remarkable variety which can characterize a single life span. Realizing their multiplicity in time, and their responsibility for every moment of it, they achieve integrity.

IV.3 ✍ THE WORD "INTEGRITY" SUGGESTS A four-dimensional morality because, unlike many other moral words, it has both spatial and temporal connotations. Spatially it implies self-sufficiency, fiber; temporally it implies persistence of spirit. We

---

* *Antony and Cleopatra*, act 4, scene 15, lines 51–55.

may infer integrity from a man's single action; but we are not sure of it until we have seen him respond to a number and variety of challenges. The word also suggests a modern morality — not because the ancients lacked it, but rather for the opposite reason: because modern man's perception of his own psychological complexity coupled with his awareness of external ambiguity and change threatens not just his sense of virtue but his sense of self. More than a virtue or group of virtues, integrity is an affirmation of self in a world where the defining outline of the individual often seems to be no more than a transparent and absorbent membrane between impersonal inner and outer forces. In such a world, the only sure sign of being is pain; the only mark of integrity an aura of trial.

IV.4 ✍ A MAN OF TWENTY, I PEEK STEALTHILY into the window of the tiny study, in Carmel Valley, California, where my older self sits writing this book. I shudder to see as reality some of the things I have feared: the wrinkles, the baldness, the ingrained mannerisms; I console myself that the figure at the desk has not grown fat, and that he is writing. I glance through other windows, wondering in spite of myself at the lack of furniture and other possessions (so old and yet so poor!); I gaze uncomprehendingly at the rosy-cheeked child, the graceful wife. I follow the writer through a few of his days, remarking dismally at their regularity, mundaneness, domesticity, lack of risk. "Is that all there is?" I ask. I yearn to rap on the window, to ask him what provoked this rejection of freedom, this submission to desolate routine. What puzzles me most of all is his appearance of being, despite his extreme age and manifest impoverishment of experience, so much happier than I have ever been.

IV.5 ✍ GROWN VERY OLD, I TURN A CORNER IN a corridor and meet, with much amazement, my younger self. He ignores me, almost walks through me, and goes hurrying off to an engagement. I follow him through an upsettingly active day. I am embarrassed by his affectations, which seem like a parody of my own more subdued mannerisms. I see myself in him, a rough confusion of traits that have since subsided into a compromise. Yet I see others in him too, glimpses of light and darkness, strangers he could have, but did not, become. His face, like a mime's, is plastic to grief and joy. His eyes continually glance outward, as though to pluck from the middle distance some wonderful secret of the future.

IV.6 ✍ JUST AS ONE SENDS A LETTER FROM PLACE to place, one may send, to one's self or others, letters through time. Photographs, mementos and journal entries are letters we send into the future; and by writing or speaking about events gone by we can communicate to some extent with the past. To do this regularly and intelligently is to expand our being in time.

IV.7 ✍ TIME IS OF COURSE THE GREATEST TEST OF integrity and one which, even at relatively short range, can produce strange results. Late at night $Herman_1$, the tired reveler, pulls off his shoes still tied and drops them over the side of the bed, leaving the proper disposition of them to his lightly regarded assistant and valet, $Herman_2$. $Herman_1$, as befits his needs and pleasures, has partaken liberally of pork and beans and drunk two quarts of ale. At 7 the next morning $Herman_2$, the morning man, crawls out of bed, belches laboriously, trips over his shoes and curses his dissolute half-brother $Herman_1$ for gross and repeated personal abuses. He resolves for the thousandth time to reform or at least curb his inconsiderate housemate and relative. These resolutions, however, will shortly be overruled and rejected by $Herman_3$, the brisk and earnest man of affairs who paces through his daily duties, arrogantly snubbing his far less distinguished housemates, and pausing now and then to consider the evening pleasures which will be his reward.

Who is the real Herman? A mathematician might answer, "Herman!" (Herman factorial) — the product of his multiplied selves, the unacknowledged totality of his permutations.

IV.8 ✍ To represent us accurately, our portraits must be painted in time as well as in space. Only then will viewers know how often the fine lips retreat into a weak smile, or the noble eyes narrow contemptuously; or whether the mass of strengths is crippled by a single weakness, or an otherwise undistinguished bundle of features is kindled by genius or made memorable by unadorned persistence. Only then will they see the massive disproportion between those of us whose awareness endures in time and those who can draw it together only for moments at a stretch. If individuals could be seen in their true four-dimensional shapes and sizes, the world would become a romance of giants and dwarfs.

IV.9 ✍ It is educational for me to be confronted (as I often am by my wife) with assertions I made in the recent past but have just contradicted as erroneous, wrongheaded or wholly insane. This momentarily gives me a healthy sense of my own motion in time, a sense of my approximate rather than absolute being, a reminder that the person I am at any given moment is neither identical to the persons of other moments nor to the larger identity which is supposed to endure through the sum of moments. It is never amiss to be reminded of one's inconsistencies, especially since hypocrisy, the champion vice, is often born of no more than inconsistency and forgetfulness.

IV.10 ✍ The components of integrity exist in most of us, elementally powerful yet scattered, unamalgamated, undiscovered. I refer not to precepts or ideals, which tend magically to evaporate at the very moment we need them, but rather to classic personal memories, so linked with intense emotion that they stand, in a sense, as material symbols of the ideal, and are available for incorporation as the bases of a coherent attitude toward experience. Like beakers of undiluted chemicals, these memories hold, in awesome purity, love, guilt, triumph, fear, anguish, relief, endurance, dignity and the whole gamut of psychological modalities which give human life its substance and depth. These memories rest latent and disconnected in everyday life. Now and then, summoned by association or necessity, one of them will leap up to serve or torment us. If, on the other hand, we could call on them at will — if we could remember daily that we draw every breath in their communal light and shadow — we would know all we needed to know about right and wrong. I have, for example, one memory of a child being seriously ill and another memory of my joy at his recovery. I have only to call up these memories for all the anxieties of my current life to shrink into convenient and portable size.

IV.11 ✒ INTEGRITY IS USUALLY SEEN AS imperviousness to fear, desire and other like emotions. But we may see it with equal accuracy as superiority to present time and to the complex of emotions whose only real existence is in the present. For all the psychological and physiological conditions which test integrity — fear, desire, hunger, fatigue, disaffection, anger, pain — have little reality in memory or anticipation but rather exist for the most part in the narrow immediacy of the present. The person of integrity is a continuous person, for whom the present is a point on a line drawn out of memory and into the willed future, rather than an unpredicted and unwieldy configuration which seems to operate under its own laws. The person of integrity is no superman; he will be, from time to time, defeated, frustrated, embarrassed and completely surprised. But neither is he the common and regular dupe of circumstance, compelled (like some tourist with a pocket dictionary) to consult conscience and emotion at each new turn of events.

IV.12 ✒ NO PSYCHOLOGICAL MESSAGE IS SO OPEN to question as that which tells us that we have nothing left to do or to give.

IV.13 ✒ IN AMERICA DURING THE 1970S, WE would hear again and again that someone or other we knew had gone through a sudden and radical emotional change, that through contact with a new philosophy or religion or adherence to a new physical regime he was simply no longer the fellow he had been, that he was disowning all past actions and launching himself on a wholly new order of life. Fortunately for the world, these changes were always perceived by their subjects as vast improvements; and nothing could attest to their salubriousness so much as the fact that, over the course of months or years, individuals would go through whole series of them, undertaking regular and total transfigurations of awareness in much the same way that eighteenth- and nineteenth-century Europeans took the waters, and infinitely enriching the army of professional redeemers who led them, again and again, to new forms of total insight.

IV.14 ✒ BINOCULAR VISION AND THE RESULTANT phenomenon of parallax allow us to form a realistic impression of three-dimensionality. Imagine for a moment having temporal parallax — simultaneous perception of two points in time separated (as our eyes are) by a relatively modest distance, 30 seconds to five minutes. Such a capacity would bring us closer to perceiving the multiple dimensionality of time; able to consider brief events both from their future and their past sides, we might appreciate them more realistically. We might ascend from our particular groove in time, viewing its objects in their fullness rather than, as is common, projections against a flat screen. Visions of this sort are impossible for us in the body, which demands that we view time as if through monocles. Less so in the mind's eye which can, through memory, reason and imagination, reconstruct the missing dimensions of phenomena.

IV.15 ✒ IT IS ESSENTIAL THAT THE LARGER SELF, which stretches across decades, should frequently make contact with the smaller self, which labors from hour to hour. Memory should be exercised consciously in bringing about these encounters. The most profound function of memory is the reflex of identity.

IV.16 ✍ A MONSTROUS FALLACY OF TIME, SO ingrained that it is almost automatic, is the idea that we necessarily learn more and more about important human experiences as time passes. Born of the metaphor of childhood and maturity or of valid educational processes like school or professional training, this idea is then applied to areas where it has no validity at all — to love, morality and politics; to art and self-knowledge. In these areas it deludes us continually about our ability to deal with events, propelling us complacently into experiences which, to our surprise, turn out to be mystifying and new. Why do we so seldom increase our knowledge of these, the important human things? Because we learn only when we can accurately remember; and we can accurately remember only when we have accurately seen and heard; and our perception of crucial events is almost always so vain and superficial and riddled with fear that we carry away little of them except the tags and wrappers.

IV.17 ✍ SUCCESSFUL PEOPLE ARE WARNED AGAINST change because it is considered unwise to alter winning tactics. Unsuccessful people are warned against change because of the danger of proliferating stillborn projects. More accurately, we may counsel the former to retain their method of achieving success, whether or not their objects change; and counsel the latter to change their method without necessarily changing their goals. Method is not (as we often think) subservient to goal but rather contains the goal within itself.

IV.18 ✍ THE FOLLOWING EXERCISES MAY BE OF some value in sharpening and renewing your sense of time:

· Buy a chess-timing clock and use it with intellectual games like chess or Scrabble. This will teach you to muster full concentration at short notice and to appreciate the riches of time that lie within comparatively short periods.
· Write an analysis of your normal day in terms of the sorts and amounts of activity it includes.

- Imagine as fully and specifically as possible what some absent friend or family member is doing at the moment.
- Focus on some period or event in the past, and try to reconstruct it in its entirety, including specific details regarding place, your relationships, pains, pleasures, hopes, fears, health, clothing — every element that contributes to a sense of the present.
- Run through the events of the past day both forward and backward.
- Conceive in detail how and where you wish to live, what you wish to know, have, be, in ten years' time.
- Describe your life up to now, as a critical but not malicious historian might, in a single paragraph.
- Describe the essence of your cultural milieu, as a sensitive but hurried historian might, in a single brief paragraph.
- Locate times of day that are regularly vacant of real activity (such as commuting, insomnia, hours after dinner) and, with the attitude of one who reclaims desert land, think of continuing mental projects which might fill them. Insomniacs, for example, should regularly address their thoughts to some difficult problem; in so doing they are likely either to solve the problem or start sleeping longer.
- Describe in writing (for your eyes only) your idea of a perfect day.
- Take some day in the past on which you know exactly where you were and what you were doing, and reconstruct it on a broader scale with the aid of old newspapers and magazines.

IV.19 ✍

> O Charmian!
> Where think'st thou he is now? Stands he, or sits he?
> Or does he walk? Or is he on his horse?*

Cleopatra thus pines for her absent Antony. Compare this cherishing with that other more prevalent form of love, vulgar and gluttonous, which simply hungers for the distant lover's return. Cleopatra's passion is so strong that it extends her identity, endowing Antony

---

* Shakespeare, *Antony and Cleopatra*, act 1, scene 5, lines 18–20.

with temporal reality even though he is not physically present. Such affection is rare in most of our lives. When we are with loved ones, we unconsciously accord them the right to exist within our own continuum of time. Once we part, this privilege is commonly revoked; and we often greet them again as if nothing had happened to them since this parting. We listen to their reports — that a son tripped on a step but did not hurt himself, that a wife ran out of gas and had to walk to the gas station — as to disparate events, divorced from natural experience or temporal continuity. And this alienation in time, whether it springs from the press of our own affairs or from selfishness or mere ignorance, is a step away from satisfying love and toward polite inhumanity.

IV.20 ⚒ DISCUSSING SHARED EXPERIENCES — past, present or future — is like looking at photographs through a stereopticon: the binocular parallax vivifies them, giving them a form of abstract and objective reality. Conversely, the sadness of a lonely life, or of a secretive life among others, is not so much that reality is painful as that it has weaker being, like some image turned on when we wake and turned off when we sleep.

IV.21 ⚒ SEXUAL BOREDOM, THAT PREDATOR OF marriages, is generally ascribed to overfamiliarity; but I think it might more aptly be blamed on the lack or failure of true intimacy. Conversely, it is not mere novelty that makes sex agreeable; were novelty the end-all, we might just as well court kangaroos. Rather, sex thrives on the dynamics between novelty and intimacy, between what is new and what is inalienably shared. To pursue these dynamics in a series of brief encounters is credible but ultimately fallacious; for brief encounters, in which little is genuinely discovered or given, tend to emphasize people's sameness rather than their individuality, and hence to obliterate the novelty that is sought. Intimacy, which demands time and trust, is available almost exclusively through marriage or long friendship. Because it is of necessity so many-faceted, because moods and characters and situations change, and because it must constantly be reestablished, intimacy brings with it forms of novelty. But intimacy — the willing revelation of self and absorption in another — is a rare thing: in the first place, because few couples ever achieve it to begin with, and in the second, because those who do tend to view it as a *fait accompli* rather than as a communal being in need of constant renewal. The typical marriage, in which love and fidelity are taken for granted, niceties omitted, disagreements hardened and defended, and understandings codified into meaningless verbal tags, can be not only less novel but less intimate than a meeting of strangers.

IV.22 ✍ TRUE INTIMACY IS A HUMAN CONSTANT. People of all types find it equally hard to achieve, equally precious to hold. Age, education, social status make little difference here; even genius does not presuppose the talent to reveal one's self completely and completely absorb one's self in another personality. Intimacy is to love what concentration is to work: a simultaneous drawing together of attention and release of energy.

IV.23 ✍ SEX MANUALS HAVE OFTEN POINTED to the lack of variety which characterizes the erotic life of the average Western adult and to the ingrained prohibitions against the enjoyment of sex at any but a few clearly-defined times and places. They imply that sex, though a permanent psychological presence, has been walled out of most daily situations and our awareness of them, constrained into brief periods and predictable attitudes which dull and diminish it. The same could be said, by projection, about many other elements of identity, crucial and intimate — affection, reverence, wonder, nostalgia, longing, indignation, humility, laughter — which we habitually isolate in small chambers of time and space, rather than understanding them as constant sources of excitement and vision.

IV.24 ✍ WHAT BREAKS UP MARRIAGES IS LESS often great shocks than conditioned reflexes of annoyance: the emotional channel so deeply grooved that it catches every flow of anger, and so securely wired to hypocritical and defensive attitudes that every challenge to our confidence is alchemized into a resentment against our mates. There is no better way to avoid this shambles of identity than to recognize, anticipate and prevent our own automatic emotional responses.

IV.25 ✍ THE HEAT OF BATTLE IS HARDLY THE best time to inform someone dear to us that he or she is a poor lover, eats repulsively or is a bore at parties; but the heat of battle is nonetheless often the time when repressed antagonism, breaking at last to the surface, seizes on such criticisms and endows them with horrific splendor. Like bloated corpses rocked to a lake's surface by cannon fire, they rise evilly into view, establishing themselves in traumatic history; and no future qualifications or denials will ever completely erase them. Conversely, other friendships are maimed by the mute resentments of people who are too frightened to speak up when angry and too lazy to do so when calm. The middle course is to endure one's grievance under stress and voice it, preferably in the form of a positive alternative, when both parties are calm and the issue is not at hand.

IV.26 ✍ THE SENSE OF CONTEXT IS AN ESSENTIAL function of thought, but also a limitation of thought; for individual contexts include only a limited range of magnitude, a tiny band along an immense range of being. Physically we are comfortable with distinctions of one or two orders of linear magnitude — a pencil or a paperclip to a desk — and oblivious at least temporarily to those natural dimensions so large as to make the desk seem subatomic, or so small as to make the paperclip seem supergalactic. By a simple analogy, this limitation in our ability to perceive broad distinctions in scope can be applied to our moral and temporal responses as well. We agonize over a dinner menu, or have engine trouble on the way to work; and for seconds or minutes our cosmos shrinks to a minuscule volume of being, an epic of cheese sauces or tragedy of fanbelts. We grow angry with a loved one;

and momentarily the rootedness of consanguinity and the magnificent sweep of past and future friendship disappear behind an existential pimple of annoyance. We can avoid such painful barbarisms by remaining aware of moral vistas which are indeed the context of context. But this breadth of vision, one must admit, is less an intellectual ability than a psychological bent, an easiness in the joints of cognition allowing for the sumultaneous awareness of things great and small.

IV.27 ✍ PLOT FOR A FILM: A MAN AND A WOMAN meet by chance in a city or town where neither of them lives. Both have had successful lives, but both are unspecifically dissatisfied with their success and honest enough to feel responsible for their own lack of contentment. After half an hour's conversation, it is clear to both that they are much attracted to each other. Both of them wish to enlarge the friendship; though each, knowing next to nothing about the other, has no idea of how much or how long this will be possible. They have not yet even exchanged names; and it occurs to the man, half fancifully but with a feeling of insight, that they should remain completely unidentified to each other. He describes his object, in terms which immediately appeal to the woman, as a relationship wholly in the present, cast off like some boat from the distracting and inhibiting influences of past and future. They have a love affair; and in the sequel the full context of time reasserts itself upon this initiative of freedom.

IV.28 ✍ TOO BUSY TO ATTEND HIS OWN WEDDING in France, the emperor Maximilian (1459–1519) sent an ambassador to the ceremony. This diplomat, having participated with the bride in the more public rites of marriage, effected a proxy consummation by placing his naked foot, duly manicured, bathed and anointed, briefly and decorously in the bed where she lay. For all its pomp and solemnity, this ritual proved ineffectual; quite soon the young woman had formed a new alliance with a more enthusiastic and portable prince. An extreme example of the fruitlessness of affection abstractly proclaimed, taken for granted, unsupported by action, unrenewed by care.

IV.29 ✍︎ EVERY HOME SHOULD HAVE A ROOM, OR at least a nook with two chairs, where it is a sin punishable by immediate expulsion to speak of money, business, politics or the state of one's teeth.

IV.30 ✍︎ LAST NIGHT I HAD A VIVID DREAM WHICH centered around the identification of one of my younger brothers (whom I remember as a tiny child) with my four-year-old son. The dream reminded me that my present feelings of paternal affection are not new to me: that they hearken back to the rudimentary feelings of protective love I had as an elder brother. Rudimentary, but intense — for the dream seemed to renew and increase my present paternal feelings, as though from some primal source. Another instance similar to this but even more compelling occurred recently when I had to leave my family in California and drive 500 miles north to begin summer school in Oregon. I was no sooner on the road than I felt submerged in totally unexpected sorrow. I realized that I had not had feelings of that sort for twenty years — not since, leaving alone for Europe after college, I said goodbye to my parents. The grieflike dejection, an intimation of final partings, had accompanied all my goodbyes to them through adolescence; but after the European adventure I did not feel it again. A grown man, I established my own home and context, free from the rooted and melodramatic interdependencies of family life. Now they were suddenly upon me again, in their full primal force — not so much as things returned to by the same road, but more as though I had come *round the other side* — as though moving along a pathway of what seemed wholly new experience I had returned amazingly to the same place. I sensed then and still feel that such haunting reconstructions are a taste of our common lot: that when we raise families, say goodbyes, grow old, we close circles in time, touching again, with unexpected wonder and pain, the nerves of our original being.

V ⚡ THE POLITICS
OF TIME ⚡ ⚡ ⚡ ⚡ ⚡

V.I ⚡ HISTORY ASPIRES AT ITS BEST TO BE A science, to examine its subjects objectively and comprehensively, through a clear glass. This aspiration, however, frequently proves to be overly ambitious; for the historian, even when he has transcended the limiting prejudices of his race, religion, nation and social class, is still beset by the prejudices of his times. Temporal prejudices are not the things we argue about but rather the things we assume — either the "truths" which seem so self-evident as not to need analysis or, more profoundly, the attitudes so thoroughly and universally internalized that they are not thought about at all. These attitudes form the bias of our vision itself; trying to question them is like trying to look through the backs of our heads. Modern capitalists and modern communists, for example, will fight to the death over the issue of how to apportion material goods; yet, underneath, both sects are materialist to the core, sharing basic assumptions which other ages would question. Western conservatives and liberals bicker over the uses of liberty; yet both share the assumption (and are here supported by the "constitutions" of communist states) that political liberty is one of the most highly prized commodities in existence. One cannot find such assumptions in Plato or Aristotle, in Matthew or Paul. Moreover, not only our blindnesses but our very strength and awareness can be sources of prejudice. Methodological virtues like the psychological or economic analysis of history can, through overemphasis, blind their possessors to realities that were obvious to earlier historians and will someday be obvious again. Historical relativists argue that, for reasons of this sort, we are totally hostage to temporal foibles; that history as a science is pure illusion. But perhaps historical relativism is itself a fallacy, most dangerous because it is so nearly true. History *would* be relative, I believe, if it did not occasionally become the province of genius — genius either so comprehensively learned that it can winnow out contemporary illusions and chronological eccentricities like chaff, exposing the common nature beneath, or genius so intensely understanding of particulars that all nonessentials are burned away in its light.

v.2   SOMETIMES WE NOTICE IN AN OLD GROUP photograph the single face of some unknown person who looks directly into our souls, suggesting some timeless form of awareness, solitary and penetrating. The intelligent student of past events undergoes a similar experience, perceiving in crowds of extraneous phenomena the solitary face of humanity: the vestige of enduring human truth which connects one age to another, one place to another, and thus saves the study of history from what would otherwise be a world of barren mechanism and formless change. More valuable yet and far rarer is the ability to perceive this face as it lies lonely and hidden in the events of one's own time.

v.3   THE IRONIC PHRASE "WISDOM OF HINDSIGHT," meaning an opinion after the event which is correct but futile, is based on the almost-universal assumption that we know more about things after they have happened than before. Surprisingly enough, however, there are reasons for doubting that this assumption is completely justifiable. After an event, we normally know at most what has happened; not what *might* have happened, had one or more of its innumerable circumstances been altered. What we "understand," in other words, is the result of a single configuration of variables, rather than the sum of what those variables were capable of producing. And we understand each circumstance only in the sense in which, conjoined with others, it produced the happening, rather than in terms of its full potentialities. Moreover, deluged in details, we miss the nobler and simpler view of forms and purposes we had when looking into the future. Finally, the fact that retrospective analyses, as opposed to prior strategies and predictions, hold little danger (they need only be plausible) often renders us more careless and self-indulgent in making them.

v.4 ✎ GENERALLY, EXPERIENCE IS ANALYZED in either of two ways: mechanistically (in terms of cause and effect) or teleologically (in terms of goal or purpose). In individual cases, one of these methods is likely to be more appropriate than the other. If we understood Booth's assassination of Lincoln teleologically, we would have to honor the murderer's pathetic illusion that he was ridding the world of a tyrant. On the other hand, if we interpreted Lincoln's great speeches mechanistically, as mere responses to political necessity, we would err just as grossly. Obviously, the blanket preference for one mode of analysis over another is to be avoided. Yet such dangerous preferences exist not only among historians (whose leaning has for some time been towards the mechanistic) but also in daily life. While most of us can weigh the mechanistic against the teleological fairly judiciously in terms of present experience, we tend, I think, to view the past mechanistically and the future teleologically. In other words, we tend to forget past purposes and to ignore future causes. This predisposition is one of the reasons why, both consciously and unconsciously, we distinguish so absolutely between past and future time. It results in faulty analyses and mistaken predictions, in a loss of moral consistency, in a failure to use memory as an effective guide to planning and, above all, in an alienation from the reality of time as continuum.

v.5 ✎ THE IDEA OF FREE WILL IN INTERACTION with mechanistic circumstance suggests no contradiction at all; for true freedom is uniquely defined by its response to the inevitable.

v.6 ✎ FOLLOWING THE SAME RATIONALE BY which, more generally, present time hogs the stage and shoulders back the other dimensions, each present age holds itself aloof from history. Although all ages march at equal pace into oblivion or the patronizing care of scholars, each age, solemnizing its own urgencies, exalts itself as unique. It proclaims itself to be the fruit of things, the ultimate product of all history: yet at the same time it informs us that it is special, that its problems are unprecedented, its perspectives radical. This is the fallacy of the end of history, the illusion by which the mandarins of a given period corrupt the masses into granting that period, however shopworn or redundant it may be, special indulgence and extreme sacrifice. It is in service to this fallacy that journalists inflate the news, that clothing shops (having already ordered the new designs that will make them outmoded and worthless) characterize present fashions as the last word, that book publishers sell yesterday's hash as a revolutionary departure. In the same vein but even more pretentious are historians who deny objectivity to any age but their own, politicians who promise a wholly new order of things, and religious zealots who proclaim themselves to be the beginning of the end. These are all the hucksters of time, the charlatans who peddle newness and are, by the same token, its worst enemies.

v.7 ✑   AS EVENTS PASS INTO HISTORY, THEY SETTLE into themselves and compose themselves in a smaller context. We forget urgent crises and all-encompassing issues and the rhetoric which, keyed profoundly to time and place, made them seem urgent and all-encompassing. These things cease to be the primal motives of action and ultimate limits of will and become instead the details of history, the geography by which we distinguish the 1960s from the 1950s, the 1980s from the 1970s. And as the whole context shrinks in the distance of time, the main outlines draw together into surprising new shapes, exposing relationships between things which seemed absurdly alien to each other during the events themselves. Allegedly radical departures reveal themselves as the children of crusty old prejudices — racial loathings, barbaric phobias and mindless interest decked out temporarily in fresh jargon and passionate righteousness. Organic ties emerge where there has seemed to be nothing but diametrical opposition — between iconoclast and establishment, persecutor and victim, right and left.

Strength and weakness, light and darkness, good and evil collapse toward each other until, in an appalling perspective, we realize that they spawned each other. The face of history smiles at us ironically, offering solace only to those who seek, in the pattern of their own frustration, the ghost of some enduring form.

v.8 ⚑ WHILE DAILY JOURNALISM PROLIFERATES itself by exaggerating emergencies and ignoring continuity, weekly journalism perverts continuity by fabricating the illusion of grand historical shape and movement. Thus we learn from a recent weekly that our President is "AT THE CROSSROADS" — a title suggesting some monumental crisis of American history. The awestruck reader is encouraged to infer first (*THE* CROSSROADS) that such a crisis has never occurred before, and second (*CROSSROADS*) that the President, who has just fired half his cabinet, apparently against his own will, and is under extreme pressure from all sides, has significant freedom of choice and action. The point, of course, is that failure to participate if only vicariously in this truly unique moment of history, especially at the modest price of $1.25, is wholly unthinkable. The editors of such journals seem to carry, like rear-view mirrors attached to long braces on their foreheads, the mystic means of seeing the present itself in the broad sweep of past and future; and this appearance becomes suspect only when we leaf through the moldy weeklies of the past to find scores of crises which even the most frenetic historians have neglected to mention, scores of crossroads which do not appear on the map at all.

v.9 ⚑ ENGLAND IS REMARKABLE FOR ITS WEALTH of local records — births, marriages, deaths, rolls, elections, fines, etc. — starting, in many cases, during the Middle Ages and preserved, in parish churches, city halls, courthouses and libraries, down to the present. This is a testament not only to the stability of English society but also to what perhaps lies behind the stability — the English sense, even on relatively humble levels, of their own dignity in time. For humanity in general the reverse seems to be true. Considering the billions of men and women who have bragged, strutted and flattered under the sun, it is remarkable how little about themselves they have left in writing. Had their records been at all proportional to their number and their self-esteem, we would have a library on every street corner, a bulging archive in every home. Instead we have a silence and emptiness so profound that family history seldom exists, in any but the most general sense, beyond living memory. The cause of this anomaly, we suspect, is not to be found in any real or imagined lack of vanity. It is rather an instinct so fundamental and pervasive that it transcends our vanity: an animal subjectivity in time which gluts solely on the present and all but obliterates the nobler vanity of our full temporal selves.

V.10 ✍ MACHIAVELLI HELD THAT POLITICAL virtue is born of crisis and can be renewed only by crisis.* He wrote that wars, revolutions and other bloody ordeals were necessary at regular intervals; because only such extreme events could terrify the people into respect for their own laws and call forth, from a few individuals, the strength necessary for effective leadership. Citing the history of the Roman Republic as his model, he recommended that states be refreshed by violence at least once every few years. Machiavelli's theory is not only shocking but also, from the perspective of twentieth-century military technology, terrifyingly impracticable. Even if a modern power could produce leaders impetuous enough to precipitate it into gratuitous conflicts, the dynamics of atomic warfare and the dangers of global destruction are so overwhelming as to render such athletic militarism impossible. But Machiavelli's underlying premise that, given human nature, undisturbed and unchallenged states grow lazy, weak and corrupt, has strong support in history and great relevance to modern times. The question of whether liberal democracy can recover, out of its own fiber and without global conflict, the spirit and vigor of its own early history, has in effect become the question of whether liberal democracy can endure at all.

---

* *Discourses,* Book III, Chapter 1.

V.II ⚹ CLASSICAL HISTORIANS SEEM TO AGREE that the roughly eighty years between the accession of Trajan and the death of Marcus Aurelius (A.D. 98–180) was a golden period of history, when the Western world, for all its diversity and change, was united under stable government and wise governors. If history holds anything at all of moral value to us, certainly this age should be discussed, dissected, questioned and compared with other ages and with our own. Yet, even though our present temper is disgusted with modern policies and fascinated by utopias of all sorts, we read and hear little about this period and other comparable periods. Why not? The world was radically different then, we claim; and even if it were not, we could not accept Trajan's assumptions, or allow ourselves to use his methods. But differences are useless and absurd except when viewed in a context which also includes similarities; and Trajan's methods and assumptions are tame and liberal indeed compared with the methods and assumptions of modern autocracies whose embassies we harbor and whose philosophies we countenance. Historical periods of the past, we retort, are of no importance except in terms of what they have contributed to the present. Yet how can we effectively understand a "contribution" when we stand not at the end of history, but rather at some intermediate point along its course? Beneath these superficial and fallacious evasions is something more visceral: an abandonment of historical and moral continuity in the face of anarchic challenge, a hypocrisy that is at once smug toward the past and terrified of the future.

V.I2 ⚹ ONE OF THE FACTORS CONTRIBUTING TO the preeminence of the ancient Greeks was their relative lack of a past. They had little accurate history to compare themselves with, few intellectual traditions to master as the prerequisites of individual inquiry. Their thinkers were not herded into arbitrary institutional stalls like "psychology," "sociology" or "political science." They were not handed down questions to answer but rather were compelled to define their questions before answering them. They were not tyrannized into conformity with doctrines for which they were not themselves responsible; nor, for the most part, were they spurred to rebel against a body of established methods or ideas. And this last point deserves special consideration: for in a way that few moderns seem to understand, the mind is as limited by what it rebels against as it is by what it accepts.

V.13 ✍ DESCRIBING WHAT HE IMPLIES TO BE A general tendency for states to decline from oligarchy through democracy to tyranny, Socrates (in Plato's *Republic*, Book VIII) details a hypothetical sequence of events which holds disquieting affinities to modern times. The fall of democracy occurs, he says, when the lower class grows weary lest the state revert to oligarchy (the prior system); and when would-be tyrants, under the demogogic pretext of saving the state from the oligarchs, win over the plebians, gain control of the state and enslave it. The endangerment of democracy in the modern world is largely due to the global strategy of the Soviets, who appeal to poor nations and the working class and who accuse the richer nations of colonialism (an earlier system resembling an international oligarchy) and the richer classes of oligarchy and monopolism. Communist revolutions, ostensibly fomented to rid nations of such conditions, characteristically enslave them.

V.14 ✍ ONE IMPLICATION OF THE PASSAGE JUST cited is that in most states political virtue, or the lack of it, is largely a function of communal memory. The people, Socrates suggests, have no basis for judging present conditions except in terms of those differing conditions which immediately preceded them. Socrates' democrats see politics merely in terms of the distinction between their system and the oligarchy which came before it; they arbitrarily assume that their own system is superior to the past. The tyrants seduce the populace through an artful misreading of both past and present. The tyrants "know" the future, at least in terms of their own desires. The people, on the other hand, have no sense of the future at all: they project it either as a continuation of the present or a reversion to the past. The conceptual bases for such a view are not hard to fill in. Most people, lacking philosophical method, strong imagination or even an objective view of the present, must fall back on memory in an effort to conceive of an alternative to the present system. Because of the propaganda of their leaders, because of the chronic myth that the present has got to be more enlightened than the past, and because of their own profound investment in current institutions real or imagined, they tend to see the prior system as something inferior if not detestable. Because of this characteristic direction of concern, they are always blindsided by the future, which bears little surface resemblance to either past or present, though it develops from currents latent in both and common to humanity.

v.15 ⚞ BEWARE OF TIMID LEADERS. EITHER their meekness will tempt enemies into depredations so severe that they can only be answered violently (and a timid man, though he may have the political power to initiate violence, has no idea at all how to use that power), or their failure to act may convince the electorate to oust them in favor of leaders so violent that they would never have been elected otherwise. Lord Acton, who informed us that "power corrupts," might well have added, by way of ironic qualification, "almost as much as impotence."

v.16 ⚞ WRITTEN HISTORY IS COMPOSED OF actions; real history is actions compounded invisibly with refusals to act.

v.17 ⚞ TYRANNY IS A THREE-DIMENSIONAL construct, an affront to motion. Constitutional democracy is an acknowledgment of four-dimensionality, an invitation to time. But constitutional democracy can protect its liberties only if it can somewhere preserve, in a world otherwise diffused with change, the wisdom which originally ensured and limited them.

V.18 ✒ VIEWED SUPERFICIALLY, PATRIOTISM IS a twofold phenomenon whose nature depends upon the times. In times of national peril, it is the simple recognition that deeply shared interests are at stake. In times of prosperity, it is the rhetoric of reaction and the language of distrustful ignorance. But rooted beneath these surface manifestations is a love of land, speech and culture so inexpressibly basic that it may be seen as an extension of instinctive self-love. And this love, though it is usually visible only through embarrassingly silly impulses and gestures, is at heart one of the few truly unifying forces of civilization and one of the few links we adults have with the natural world and the unalloyed affections of children. Intellectuals distrust patriotism not because they are more intelligent than others but rather because they have been taught in a thousand ways to distrust all their basic emotions.

V.19 ✒ TIME IS THE HIDDEN QUALIFIER OF ALL political thought and can assert itself with such silent emphasis as to turn some theories completely upside-down. Liberalism, for example, was born in the myth of the Golden Age, when people were supposed to have lived happily without laws or rulers. It follows from this that government was not a natural phenomenon but rather an imposition on nature; government therefore "owes" something to the people whose freedom it has unnaturally taken away. This debt to the people was originally conceived (Locke, Rousseau) as being political liberty — liberty, that is, limited by reason and guaranteed by law. But in more recent years this debt has been either wholly replaced (Marx) by a debt of material, or else enlarged (European socialism) to include both freedom and material security, or else even more ambitiously expanded (the United States) to include freedom, material security and special rights for the disadvantaged. These modern ramifications of liberalism, however different from each other, all call for government on a massive scale — government that protects, controls, provides. In this way political theory based on the distrust of government has evolved into the provender for behemoths of government.

V.20 ✍ ONE OF THE GREAT MODERN POLITICAL fads — so much a fad that it still strikes listeners as a sign of profound enlightenment — is to blame something on the system. It is not the criminal, we say, who corrupts society, but rather society which creates the criminal; and, analogously, society has disenfranchised the elderly, made the poor poor and benighted the ignorant. This view of social responsibility has bases in truth: for people derive a good deal of their character from the social circumstances they are born into and, moreover, many of the world's more top-heavy governments have injustice written into their very constitutions. But as an arbitrary habit of mind, the idea is ridiculous. It is a comprehensive denial of individual responsibility: not only the responsibility of acting virtuously oneself, but the responsibility for judging the good or bad actions of others. It teaches the young that everything they find wrong with life, everything they do poorly or refuse to do at all, every boredom, excess or error, is someone else's fault. Instead of facing real evils, it lays the blame on a convenient abstraction, so shadowy and distended that it cannot be held accountable. It ignores the fact that free societies, which are configurations of individual wills and which bend with the varying pressures of historical necessity, inevitably nurture particularized injustices; and that the only conceivable way of eliminating these particular injustices would be a government so absolute as to be a universal injustice. It counsels us to avoid the painful necessity of healing, or at least binding and patching, the parts of our society which hurt.

V.21 ✍ LIKE TODDLERS, WHO WITH FIERCE instinct seek alternately their own freedom and the safety of their mothers' arms, we go through life spicing our security with liberty and buttressing our liberty with security. We are like kites, which would fall except for the strings that hold them to earth; like tops, whose stability is impracticable without motion. Our lives are, at their best, patterned to accommodate this antithetical but complementary balance of desires. This balance is evident in much that we love and admire: in nature, in religion, in great art and the laws of great republics. It should be copied in our attitude toward career and retirement, the design of our houses, our relationships with loved ones and the living pattern of our day.

V.22 ✍ COMMON LANGUAGE OFTEN SEEMS TO associate good fortune intimately with the idea of time. Note the French *heureux*, the Latin *secundus*, and the German *selig*, all temporally based words having to do with good luck. Yet it is hard to verbalize this relationship. What does language know that we do not? An idiomatic definition of luck, "Being in the right place at the right time," may provide us with the beginning of an answer.

Take, for example, the pass interception in football. Interceptions characteristically result from errors on the part of the passer or receiver and hence cannot be "planned" by the interceptor. This fact makes the interception a prime example of luck in athletics. Yet some defensive players are luckier than others and amass great tallies of interceptions. Analysts associate the luck of these players with good positioning. Good interceptors have the art of reading almost instantaneously the direction of a play as it takes shape and of moving into positions where they will be most likely to prevent or minimize offensive gains. In these positions they are also most likely to be where errant passes drop. In this combination of art and fortune they seem to bear out the old saying that "fortune is the residue of design." One cannot plan to be lucky; but sensible planning and action make one accessible to luck.

V.23 ✍ THE PLAY OF JACK NICKLAUS AT HIS best is a classic example of the proper attitude toward hard times and good times. In difficult positions he plays conservatively, preferring the loss of a single stroke to the chance of losing more. Once out of danger he hits aggressively and takes risks for birdies. He understands that boldness, a great virtue in prosperity, is a great vice in adversity. And, prosperous or unlucky, he never rushes a shot. In these and other ways his instinct for good golf is so profound and complete that his game is like a small image of a life well lived. Similar precepts can be inferred from the tactics of football coaches who make their teams play conservatively after reversals of fortune (except when there is little time) and basketball coaches who slow down the action (either with ball control or times out) when their opponents are rallying. Such coaches realize that the easiest way to prolong bad luck is to try to compensate for it frenetically; that luck favors the *pro* and not the *contra;* that the wisdom of misfortune is patience and care.

v.24 🖎 MACHIAVELLI (in *The Prince*) AND BACON (in "Of Fortune") both teach that unscrupulous people tend to be lucky; both see such people as psychologically more flexible and in tune with changing times. Perhaps this sad opinion was more pertinent to their age, when governments tended to be autocratic and political stability was tenuous, than to our own. Modern liberal democracies are open and prize honesty; they are stable and prize consistency; they distrust political chameleons and seldom grant them major success. Our democratic vice is not to reward unscrupulousness but rather to exalt mediocrity. Besides, even when unscrupulous individuals have succeeded, they have seldom been able to appreciate their success. How can they feel security when their response to experience must remain so variable with circumstance? How can they be invulnerable to fortune and remain open to love?

v.25 🖎 STILL, MANY OF US BELIEVE, THOUGH we may not often admit it, that bad people tend to be more successful than good people. Consoling ourselves with wine and fellowship, we lament this knavish upward mobility and blame it on the way of the world. Such opinions are, I think, rather hard on the world and rather easy on ourselves. In the first place, there are fewer really bad people than most of us tend to believe. Successful individuals are generally no less scrupulous than average men and women: the difference is that the former have been tempted, while the latter have never had the chance to fall. Successful people are thus not demonstrably "worse" than others; and indeed, since success seldom comes to those who lack energy, technical skill and personability, they are arguably superior. Secondly, people who lack success but are reputed "good" often suffer from the weaknesses which go hand in hand with their virtues: timidity cohabiting with gentleness, reticence with honesty, prudishness with rectitude. Their virtue is more an adamant refusal to do wrong than an urgent initiative toward right. They possess the Christian virtues we all praise but lack the Roman virtues, the courage and aggressiveness, that would in proper proportion give them moral fullness. They are, to use Winston Churchill's phrase, sheep in sheep's clothing. Their lack of success, though it may be the world's loss, is not the world's fault; it is their own.

v.26 ✍ I N *The Merchant of Venice,* SHAKESPEARE gives us an idea of what it means to be truly lucky. Bassanio, who courts and wins the beautiful and wealthy Portia, is carefree, sanguine, jovial and unembarrassed by his own pursuit of wealth. He is a pleasant but by no means unusual young man, ordinary except for his curious attitude toward fortune. Just as he chooses a dangerous and unlikely courtship and a dangerous means of carrying that courtship on (borrowing heavily), he wins the trial of the caskets (act 3) by making the most menacing and improbable choice: the leaden casket ("which rather threaten'st than dost promise aught") over the silver and the gold. Students of luck can draw only one conclusion from Bassanio's example: to be lucky, one must not only dare the odds but love the odds. This is not an endorsement of compulsive gambling. The compulsive gambler, who not only risks a little to gain a lot but also risks a lot to gain a little, is not a lover of great ventures but a jaded soul in need of stimulation. It is rather an endorsement of the individual who is sensitive to that improbable magic by which life conceals its true goodness in shoals of danger and barrens of disrepute.

v.27 ✍ SUPERSTITIOUS PEOPLE HAVE TOLD ME that they are, in general, luckier than those of us who try to be sensible and realistic; and I have not the slightest reason to disagree. As I see it, their success depends less on "luck" as we commonly understand it than on a much more solid human basis. All trappings of superstition — the charms, the incantations, the generalized rubbing of dice — suggest that their practitioners sincerely respect that chronic aspect of things which is uncontrollable and unknowable, those fine interweavings of circumstance which can suddenly reverse the flow of good or bad times. This humility and openness toward luck encourages a talent for enduring bad times and tempering our vanity in good times; it breeds a dissociated readiness for new things, which approximates, as much as anything does, the talent of being lucky. The lover is better for having loved, even if he is not loved in return; the man who prays is better for having humbled himself, even if he has prayed to empty space. Similarly, the individual who respects fortune, even if it is only a mechanistic concatenation of circumstance, shows himself capable of enduring it and enjoying it.

v.28 ✍ OMNIA, LTD., THAT DYNAMIC CONGLOMERATE, has in the past two months dropped from 70 to 8 and now is more or less stabilized at 10¾. Mr. Neumann, who owns 1,000 shares, sells out. Neumann, who was hoping to sell the stock in six months at 100 and buy into avocados, is just plain disgusted and wishes to salvage what he can. Mr. Altschul also owns 1,000 shares of Omnia, but does not for a moment consider selling them. He realizes that the new value of 10¾ is as putative and unstable as the old value of 70. He expects that, sooner or later, the stock will be considered a bargain and rise again. Besides, he had no specific plans to do anything with the stock at a given date. Altschul not only does not sell; he blithely puts the apparent disaster out of his mind and accepts his newly diminished position as the basis for future speculation. On the face of things, Altschul is the wiser of the two investors. More importantly, his behavior suggests certain axioms regarding good fortune: One does not establish a calendar for one's future good luck. One does not evaluate one's own position in terms of what has just been lost, but rather in terms of what remains to work with. One does not, out of anger or panic, reject completely those associations that have proven to be unfortunate; for usually some good remains in them, and the good that remains is usually more solid and promising than the good that has been lost. One preserves, not passionately but with the care of an archivist, the bits and tatters of one's prior loves; for almost everything that has been good in the past can be good again in the future.

V.29 ⚹ PEOPLE INSTINCTIVELY REGARD their good luck as something they have deserved and their bad luck as something they have not. In so doing they misconceive the nature of luck and run afoul of it. Luck has nothing at all to do with the past. It is a whisper from the future, to be enjoyed only by those who cherish the futurity within themselves.

V.30 ⚹ THE NEW IS FOREVER NEW, BUT our powers to appreciate it quickly weaken and age. The new is forever the same, but our language for understanding it changes with the shadows. The truth is forever the same, forever new.

VI ✒ MORALITY
IN TIME ✒ ✒ ✒

VI.1 ✒   TIME IS THE INDWELLING MYSTERY OF
right action, and temporal awareness is what delineates wisdom
from the mechanistic response to circumstance. If it were not for
time, a few lines of Immanuel Kant, ringing with mathematical
justice, would make us all good people. But the persistent erosion
and fertilization of time mock even the most sensitive verbal calcu-
lus and grind down the sharp edges of thought, muddying distinctions and confusing contraries. Caught in this flow we abandon
the grand and innocent abstractions — knowledge, justice, integrity,
courage — in search of humbler but more durable goals — imagination, vigilance, tolerance, generosity, endurance. We forsake our
quest for fixed interrelationships, listening instead for a subtle and
almost ghostly music of experience, an undertone of cycles and
rhythms and recurrences, which alone seems to possess an enduring relationship to nature.

VI.2 ✒   AN AXIOM WHICH SEEMS IMPLICIT IN
almost every traditional moral code is that every action has a consequence. A second axiom, more debatable but nonetheless intrinsic
to this study, is that action is continuous. Action, in other words,
includes what we commonly call inaction; and consequence springs
as much from our refusal to act as from our willed deeds themselves. We are, then, as answerable for our temporal vacancies as
we are for our temporal substance; and time keeps nothing with as
deadly care as the ledger of our omissions. This is nowhere as ap-

parent as in our personal relationships. We lose what is valuable in these — love, joy, communality — less through conflict and tragedy than through long series of shadowy and often unconscious refusals. Withdrawing, forgetting, falling out of touch, ignoring or avoiding or withholding the unpretentious but essential details of friendship, destroy more relationships than death or anger and tend to isolate their perpetrators quite early in the solitary confinement of old age. To the Latin adage *Qui tacet consentit* ("He who is silent consents"), we might add another, *Qui non agit negat* ("He who does not act, denies").

VI.3 ✍ THE ANCIENTS WEIGHED THE achievement of an individual by the sum and substance of his actions. Most of Plutarch's biographies — for example, of Themistocles, Alcibiades, Pompey and Antony — are heroic assortments of virtues and vices, clear renderings of the psychological diversity and paradox which seem almost indispensable components of historic greatness. We moderns, on the other hand, influenced by our religion, qualify all our estimation with a surgical standard of moral purity. For the ancients, virtue was action, accomplishment, contribution; for us it is an essence so pure and fragile in nature that a beaker of goodness can be ruined by a dram of sin. Dante makes his beloved teacher, Brunetto Latini, a sufferer in hell, because all his memorable virtues were combined with a single serious vice. Francis Bacon is almost never mentioned as an historical figure without reference to the single act of malfeasance which, deftly exploited by an enemy, ended his political career. The grievous and numerous faults of Winston Churchill are expounded upon interminably by the beneficiaries of the free institutions he fought to save. And this stubborn altruism, often so extreme as to constitute a conspiracy against nature, extends beyond our histories into our daily lives. Shunning peccadillos, we suffer infamies. Anxious to avoid even appearing to do harm, we lose touch with the necessarily hazardous practice of goodness. We use rectitude to mask our envy of achievement.

VI.4 ✑ WE ARE INJURED, BUT SHRINK FROM response; we are insulted, but the reply sticks in our throat. We must choose between two manifestly imperfect candidates, and we refuse this choice, unaware that we ought not merely to vote for the less imperfect, but also to stump for him. We see the greater part of the world polluted by rats and flies, by ideological piracies so ravenous and cynical that they barely deserve the name politics; yet we hang back, wary of the disaster, guilt or humiliation which may result from moral action. We are victims of our own virtue — of Judeo-Christian virtue, which is better at shunning evil than it is at doing good; of liberal virtue, which espouses a tolerance so radical that it encourages the enemies of liberty and tolerance. The vice of these virtues is delay — endless debates and miscellaneous adjustments whose sole psychological purpose is to obscure the simple necessity for action. And the armor of this vice is a conspiracy of self-righteousness so ironclad as to stifle controversy. Devastating reversals, due in large part to our own impotence, are seen as tests of integrity, successfully passed. Waist-deep in rubble, we praise each other's fairness and forbearance. Our frustrated outrage, largely withheld from our enemies, is heaped on those few compatriots who have the impudence to suggest positive action in self-defense. Justly so perhaps: the enemy merely exploits us, but these scoundrels insult our morality.

VI.5 ✑ THE RAREST AND DEAREST COMPONENTS of moral virtue are memory and courage. Lacking these, though they may have every other blessing of culture, people are but sheep. The sheepish code, moreover, often condemns courage as belligerence and memory as reaction.

VI.6 ✑ CHRISTIANITY TEACHES THAT JUSTICE IS absolute, regardless of circumstance. Machiavelli, who would not in this or other respects have minded the title of Antichrist, advanced the opposite argument, that circumstance was the sole basis and arbiter of action. Most of us seek some form of compromise between these polarities. Aristotle taught differently about virtue. The Aristotelian "mean" was no compromise, but rather a state so different from either polarity that it was in essence the opposite of *both* polarities. Claiming that both Christians and Machiavellians totally misread experience, the modern Aristotelian would urge his followers to behave themselves in such a way that Christians denounced them as Machiavellians and Machiavellians denounced them as Christians. Such a rationale is the general subject of this chapter. Obviously one of my goals is to counteract, on moral and political levels, the ill effects of altruism on the one hand and opportunism on the other. More essentially, it is to perform morally in the same way that Machiavelli's contemporary, Michelangelo, said he performed artistically: to seek the statue in the stone — to find and hold, from the changing flow of circumstance, the inborn principles of nature.

VI.7   CHRIST AND MACHIAVELLI, WHILE differing in almost every major respect, held in common one precious secret about the nature of reform. Both realized that the individual who is concerned about the vices of a given culture must begin by attacking its apparent virtues.

VI.8   THE PROBLEM OF ACTIVE VIRTUE IS NOT so much doing the right thing as learning to repeat it. As amateur athletes and musicians know well, having done something right once is no guarantee of being able to repeat it, much less being able to do it at will. There are in fact three stages in the development of virtue: (1) the conscious experience of right action as a discrete phenomenon, (2) the ability to perform such action whenever we wish, and (3) the internalization of right action to the extent that, ceasing to be performed on impulse, it becomes a kind of impulse itself. This final stage, coherent with the classical idea of temperance, might be regarded by some moderns as an unattractive kind of psychological automation, an abdication of awareness and free choice. The ancients would reply that, on the contrary, temperate individuals, having transcended the minor annoyances and dilemmas of moral life, are uniquely free to exercise their will regarding matters of real importance. They can practice real humanity, leaving the rest of us, figuratively, to pick our noses and scratch at fleas.

VI.9 ✍ THE GRAY ZONE BETWEEN FREEDOM AND necessity, the median which partakes of both but can be identified fully with neither, is habit. The habitual act bespeaks a free choice on the part of the agent, but its implications are not free because the agent has, in a sense, chosen not to choose, but rather to relax into a graven channel of behavior. This ambiguity is critical and often tragic because, if we consider them closely, we see that most moral issues involve habit rather than freedom or necessity pure and simple. If it were common, for example, for individuals to get drunk once and then forswear the bottle, to commit a single crime and then permanently reform, or to seize power and voluntarily give it up, moral inquiry would be a precise science and we could mainly leave our doors unlocked at night. But just as such actions tend to spring from long-repressed desires, they also extend their shadows far into the future where, as Macbeth found out, they assert themselves as principles and lay claim to all time. For these reasons, moral inquiry must concern itself not with "free" will alone but also with will as solidified in habit; and moral teaching must not only develop the intellective faculties but also incise the proper grooves of habit.

VI.10 ✍ PEOPLE WHO MAKE MORAL COMPROMISES in order to achieve good ends find that their compromises irrevocably alter the ends achieved. Thus they learn that, in a world of process, it is method rather than goal which carries the burden of moral value; that in the final analysis nothing should be mistaken either for a means or for an end. Other people, who adhere to righteous action with no regard for the consequences, are equally off the mark; these people mistake method itself for an end and act as though in a vacuum of time.

VI.11 ✍ WE TEND TO SEE OPPORTUNISTS AS
hard-hearted villains who meticulously calculate every action in
the light of self-interest. But in fact there are relatively few people
who are so thoroughly bad. Run-of-the-mill opportunists calculate
little if anything and tend to lead more disorganized lives than normal people. They often think of themselves as weak, lacking in
purpose or beset by unfortunate circumstance. They do not advance into opportunity so much as take refuge in it. Their lives are
one general and subdued state of emergency; and the pattern of
self-serving action we revile is for them no pattern at all, but rather
a series of unpremeditated adjustments to what they conceive as
necessity. They regard the discomforts they inflict on others, when
at all, as small compared with their own sufferings. In this they are
probably correct.

VI.12 ✍ BOLD PEOPLE CAN ONLY WITH GREAT
effort be patient and must admonish themselves to be merciful. But
timid people, though they may pride themselves on their patience
and mercy, have not the slightest idea what either word means.

VI.13 ✍ THE BASIC LAWS OF SOCIAL
interdependence command us, among many other things, not to
be injured, duped, jilted or otherwise diminished in any way serious enough to make us the habitual recipients of support and sympathy from our fellows. Centuries of Christianity and decades of
liberal neglect for moral issues may have blurred our awareness of
this necessity, but it nonetheless asserts itself in effect as much as
ever. A perennial victim is as great a drag on society as a perennial
rascal, and in his own way is equally corrupt. Moreover, while we
may hate and chide the rascal at will, we feel compelled to love the
victim, an unnatural undertaking which makes him more bother-
some still.

How do we learn this ancient but very un-Oriental art of self-
defense? By studying, first of all, the ways of evil.

VI.14 🖎 JEWISH TRADITION, FOLLOWED BY ST. Augustine, teaches that goodness is substance and evil is void. This distinction is most pertinent psychologically: for while goodness implies to most of us wholeness and integrity, evil behavior can never be dissociated from some lack or need. We associate evil with people who take things not officially their own, who gratify themselves excessively and illegitimately, who act in fear of some imaginary danger, or who feel toward humanity in general a homogeneous sense of outrage and desire for revenge. Thus the evil man is inevitably an active man, taking and consuming, guarding and attacking. Here lies the characteristic paradox of good and evil: for action, in terms of practical effects, is superior to inaction, and the congenitally active evil man can frequently win advantage over the sometimes inactive good. Indeed, the fundamentally stable and restful spirit of goodness is a lure to evil inspirations, an encouragement to villains who are aware that, in the moral and political chess game, they have the white pieces and the first move.

VI.15 🖎 UNSCRUPULOUS INDIVIDUALS AND governments have a special genius and characteristic insight into the ways of time. Unlike the rest of us, they seem intuitively to *see* and *feel* time, as the light and shadow, the stress and limpness, which can alternately expose and conceal, prevent and allow their misdeeds. They play with time, to use an unholy comparison, in much the same way that jazz musicians play with a theme: seizing the upbeat, syncopating their actions to avoid open conflict with the metronomic plodders who are their potential victims or pursuers. In the passages which follow (VI. 16–20) I summarize a number of these villainies of time.

VI.16 🖎 THE FOURTH DIMENSION IS THE NATIVE medium of evil. Villains traditionally love the night because it obscures their deeds; but no darkness obscures things as effectively as time. We steal and eat our neighbor's goose; but these paltry facts, these negligible carbuncles on the face of history, in no way prevent us from having assured him beforehand that we would not steal it, afterward that we did not steal it, and forever that we are simply not that sort of fellow. In all these cases time is our friend, for the future conceals our intentions, and the past obliterates their results. Time fills victim, prosecutor and jury with doubt; time slowly erodes their sense of outrage. And while they look for person and deed in vain, we disperse our separate and various actions over the calendar; we dance in and out of the foliage of days, showing an eye here, a hand there, never the full self. They seek us, and they find us not.

VI.17 ⚘ VILLAINS GRAND OR PETTY ARE remarkably adept at making hasty retreats from positions in which they have been vigorously attacked. The scrupulous person, caught in some false position, generally struggles like an upended beetle; the villain miraculously vanishes in an octopodal cloud of excuses, disclaimers and assurances. He will call it an accident, or a misunderstanding; he had been led to believe otherwise; he was under duress; he did not know it mattered; yes, we understand each other now; it's settled for good. He will sidle up to you as if he and you were moral twins, and will commiserate with you about the ironies of circumstance and the silly ways of the world. And in so doing he will be beating you twice: once by deluding you about history, and once by capitalizing, for his own safety, on your inbred distaste for making trouble. But for all this consummate skill at moral posturing, the villain never seems to learn the most graceful and effective form of retreat, the art of simple apology. Perhaps he is afraid that, by admitting a little, he would imply the admission of everything. Perhaps he is, beneath his smoothness, so angry and self-righteous that the thought of apology is anathema. Perhaps apology implies the thought he can least accept, least endure: the fact of his own responsibility.

VI.18 ⚘ MOST PEOPLE AND NATIONS, WHOSE normal instinct is to avoid pain and trouble, are slow to suspect evil intentions and, if properly placated, quick to forget evil deeds once done. Hitler at first disguised brutal aggression as justifiable nationalism. Later, after each step in his conquest of most of Europe, he successfully assured the rest of the world that he intended to proceed no further.

A *fait accompli* causes less furor than an anticipated or revealed intention. Russia rolled tanks into Prague in 1968, *then* debated the moral significance of this action with the rest of the world.

When complete actions are impossible to achieve without conflict and infamy, one may instead work gradually, allowing each increment of villainy to harden into a *status quo* and achieving enormous crimes by steps which individually are not provocative enough to trigger a massive reaction. When the Nazis took over Amsterdam, they saw to it that the Jewish population, an integral and respected element of the city, was first isolated; then, in slow steps, disenfranchised, imprisoned and destroyed.

Gratuitously fomented minor crises keep one's opponents off balance. While your actions are planned and purposed, theirs are incoherent and lamed by surprise.

VI.19 ✒ VILLAINS TAILOR THEIR DEEDS TO what is allowable at the moment; their words, to what is believable at the moment. One is as bad as one can safely be, as good as one can credibly seem. Even the most outrageous lies can, through steady repetition, gain a kind of unholy seniority. They may never be believed, but at least they will cease to shock.

People who have not recently been enslaved, and people who have not recently been free, tend equally to lose touch with the distinction between these two conditions.

Given the choice between action and delay, people will generally delay.

Free states and scrupulous individuals see life in terms of stability, prolonged by law and changed, if at all, by measured progress.

Their unscrupulous counterparts see life as constant and indefinite agitation. The latter understand that the former's dislike of change can be turned into a tactical disadvantage.

VI.20 🔏 FREE STATES CHARACTERISTICALLY attempt to restrain aggressive tyrannies through rational negotiation. Aggressive tyrannies understand the essential absurdity of such negotiation, but nonetheless participate in it with enthusiasm, knowing that it will camouflage their intentions and win them time.

Negotiating with wronged people, one turns the subject of conversation from the correction of past wrongs to the prevention of future wrongs.

Good liars take pains to tell the truth as often and as eloquently as possible. When they cannot tell the truth, they concoct fictions which are subtle perversions of obvious fact. When they must prevaricate outright, they base their lies on factors which do not exist in the present, but rather require either memory or prophecy to substantiate.

The world reserves its greatest opprobrium for crimes which fail; while oblivion grows over successful misdeeds like grass over graves. It more readily forgives a wrongdoer who harms it occasionally but generally leaves it in peace than it forgives the courageous individual who regularly warns against evil.

VI.21 🔏 IT IS NOT ENOUGH TO RECOGNIZE THAT these theorems of evil exist; we must recognize that they exist *in time,* that they are natural elements of social intercourse and will be, forever, repeated, varied and reinvented. We are thus confronted with the disquieting realization that, if we honor the idea and practice of goodness at all, we must undertake and persist in the awareness of evil in all its forms. We cannot understand or preserve the substance of life without also understanding the void. Evil, in all its complexity and subtlety, must be included in an even more complex and subtle view which is not evil. Moreover, we cannot effectively relegate this awareness to a group of specialists — ombudsmen or soldiers or policemen or politicians — in order to leave our own minds free of stress. For these specialists, by the nature of their concentration, will necessarily lack the total view and be unable to direct their actions providently; while we, also lacking the total view, will be equally unable to direct the specialists. We must therefore accept the study of evil, painful and oppressive as it is, as an indispensable component of freedom — a freedom which, contrary to usual belief, is best characterized by the unpleasant and inexorable demands it makes upon us.

VI.22 ✒ THE STRONG ARE FREE TO TRUST, THE weak constrained to.

VI.23 ✒ INGRATITUDE AND BAD FAITH ARE THE simple functions of time and ignorance; for it is difficult to remember need from the vantage point of satiety, and common for the ignorant to view their obligations as arising from promises made by other people in other worlds.

VI.24 ✒ THE REASON SO MANY PROMISES ARE not kept is the same as the reason they are made in the first place.

VI.25 ✒ BY NATURE WE FORGIVE AND FORGET A whole zoo of petty injuries; but we seldom forget, and have trouble forgiving, being lied to. In a curious sense, an injury is once, a lie forever.

VI.26 ✒ THE MOST EPIDEMIC AND RECURRENT of crimes, though one seldom punishable by law, is the sweet and

sociable offense of slander. What complex of malice provokes habitual slanderers to action is, unless we are trying to cure ourselves
of this vice, scarcely worth the trouble to determine. It is enough
to be able to deal with them; and to do so we must map their stra-
tegic context. Slander cannot thrive without three basic conditions: (1) apparent friendship between slanderers and their audience,
(2) prevalent reluctance of the audience to expose the slander and
its origin to the victim, and paradoxically (3) apparent friendship
between slanderers and their victims. This third and most important condition inheres for two reasons: (1) because an audience is
unlikely to believe (and hold as a confidence) an accusation made
against an avowed enemy, and (2) slanderers are by nature afraid
of open enmity. If they had any taste for frank criticism or open
expression of grievance, they would not be slanderers at all. This
last condition suggests the slanderer's major tactical weakness. Once
alerted, the victim need only advertise his lively and comprehensive disaffection with the slanderer; in so doing the victim effectively destroys the circumstances which give rise to slander and
make it believable.

VI.27 ✎ AMONG THE AVOWED PURPOSES OF
criminal justice are (1) to educate the offenders, (2) to serve as an
example to potential offenders, (3) to prove to the rest of society
that its safety and values are being defended and (4) to maintain,
insofar as possible, a conformity between equity as perceived and
equity as practiced. But none of these is the primary purpose,
which is to make the bastards stop doing what they are doing. The
extent of crime — indeed its very nature — depends on harm threat-
ened or inflicted; arresting the criminal is essential chiefly because
it arrests the harm. We should shut the gates first and worry about
the damages later: society, like anything else attacked in nature,
should defend itself before fighting back. For this reason alone is
harshness in enforcement and punishment justified. Conversely, law-
yers who use every loophole to free their clients, and judges who
allow this, are culpable, not so much because they often protect
criminals as because they characteristically protect crime and insti-
tutionalize disorder.

VI.28 ✍ IN THE HILLS SOUTH OF GRANADA, ALONG the road to Motril, there is a spot known as El Suspiro del Moro (The Moor's Sigh). It is the last place where the southward traveler can look back on the distant city. The legend is that Boabdil, the last Moorish ruler of Granada (he signed it over to Ferdinand in 1491), resting here on his final departure from the city, looked back and sighed with regret. His wife scolded him for this and told him that he should have expressed his distaste for losing Granada much earlier, while there was still hope of saving it. Like the Moor, we are often the victims of poor timing: of saying or doing the right thing at the wrong time and of saying or doing nothing at the right time. Conversely, we must often endure the sensible advice or spontaneous affection of others at times when we are unable to appreciate these expressions, and find such bounties strangely lacking when we need them.

Indeed, there are two times for most important statements or actions: the *expressive* time, when we feel inwardly impelled to say or do them, and the *impressive* time, when they would be most helpful to their recipients. It is only in very mature and rightly beloved people that these two times regularly coincide.

For example, we generally have a volcanic attitude toward our own intrafamily annoyances and frustrations, not expressing them openly until they have grown so strong that it is impossible either to put them sensibly or hold them back. The eruption usually either provokes or occurs during a family squabble, when all parties involved have lost their tempers or are scared stiff. At these times no one listens carefully, and criticisms are exaggerated; we tend to characterize the actions which upset us, not as temporary and reparable failings, but as the products of ingrained vice or genetic debility. Thus expressed, our anger not only fails to correct disorder but rather becomes an injury which prolongs it. To say that we lack self-control is not enough. What we lack is the courage and providence to have expressed ourselves sooner.

VI.29 ✍ IT IS NOT DISSIMILAR WITH THE expression of love. We generally save this for special occasions, forgetting that love, which is the most precious form of human sustenance, is needed daily. We tend to grow amorous when *we* need

love rather than when we sense that others need it. We are upset
and annoyed by another person's request for our love, feeling that
it insults our emotional integrity; when in fact it is usually a
healthy invasion of the coldness and distance which guard our
egocentric lives. Victims of a romantic illusion which is itself a
form of selfish crudeness, we ignore the fact that love can and
should be offered by the mind and will as well as by the inspired
emotions. By omitting the regular expression of love, we alienate
ourselves from the common channels of understanding and sympathy with our fellows, and thus indeed with the sources of inspired emotion as well. We would do well to remember that small
children, who express love and appeal for it many times each day,
are in this not different from our own inner selves.

VI.30 ✍ BUT PERHAPS OUR GREATEST DRAWBACK
with regard to human timing is that we are chronically behind-
hand in our actions. It may be for this reason that, with countless
fictional heroes and heroines at their disposal, modern individuals
so frequently identify with Shakespeare's Hamlet. *Hamlet* is the
only Shakespearean tragedy in which the definitive action (here,
Claudius' murder of Hamlet's father) takes place *before* the opening scene. This fact imposes on the whole drama a frustrating mechanical causality, an aura of action as response rather than initiative. Hamlet, the central victim and symbolic embodiment of this
frustration, is at once denied freedom and compelled to act. He is
thus a premonition of modern life, in which the individual, be-
sieged by dozens of major and minor issues each day, comes to see
action as a series of adjustments to circumstance rather than a
creative instrument. The typical complaint of the modern middle
class, as ingrained and automatic as hello and thank you, is that
they are harassed and bedeviled by hundreds of routine demands.
It is significant that we normally respond to this complaint with
equally automatic sympathy, rather than regarding it critically as
a defect of vision and will. We have gotten so used to looking at
time's rear end that we no longer realize that it has another side
as well. We rightly see life as a series of challenges but do not see
that, in a more profound sense, it is also a series of preparations.

VII ⚘ PSYCHOLOGICAL TIME ⚘ ⚘ ⚘ ⚘ ⚘ ⚘ ⚘

VII.1 ⚘ MY SON ANTHONY, TAKING ME FOR walks through the high grass and unpruned shrubs of our lot in Carmel Valley, will always lead me into little dells, green rooms formed by the lowest branches of the Monterey pines or Monterey cypresses that grow along the borders of the property—with much delight, as though in those wild and removed but personal and cosy places we can start a new and secret life, free of household routine and built on the green and sunny laws of a different world. And I remember living out, with equal delight, my own versions of pastoral when I was Anthony's age, first in Fair Haven, then in Rumson, New Jersey. Later, at around 11, I developed a more ambitious nook, called Huckleberry Heaven, atop a vine-covered tree behind our house on Fox Hill in Little Silver; and still later I taught my younger brothers to climb a similar tree behind the house in Red Bank where my parents still live. We would scramble up the old trees, sit on the vine-upholstered benches that were their tops, munch on berries and otherwise do nothing. Here we developed, most uncharacteristically for us, a love of total idleness, a taste for enjoying, silent and motionless, the isolated and retarded time which rose all around us like a new element in the warm stillness. These were for us excursions into space-time, spatial nests of time where physical circumstance made time gentle, dreamy and intimate, separating it from all other experience. Such pleasant nests, available to those who live on the distant planet of youth, are forbidden to us older ones. Even if we succeed in removing ourselves from the world, we cannot (in Montaigne's words) remove the world from ourselves. But with some concentration and stubbornness we can establish for ourselves another sort of nest in time, a refreshing period of solitude or conviviality sanctified by regularity and guarded like sacred ground.

VII.2 ✍ WHEN I SPEAK OF A NEST OF TIME, I mean any frequently repeated experience whose unique dynamics, intensity of involvement and regular length wall it off from other experiences and so establish a discrete psychological environment. While we habitually seek out nests in space, areas for privacy or intimacy or repose, we are relative novices in establishing these temporal havens, and slow in realizing that free space is useless without uncluttered time. Indeed, a nest of time need not require a special place at all: its only two requirements are that it concern some desirable activity and that it be, barring emergencies, inviolable. A writer sits down to work. It is nine in the morning, and the next four hours are free, just as they have been the day before and will be the day after, by his express decision and unequivocal need. He looks down those four hours as down a clear view of unencumbered space; more broadly, the regular work periods of the future open up like a long bright hallway of work in freedom. He has no need to fear a wasted hour, an unproductive day, and conversely he has no time-related excuse for sloth or failure. Two lovers meet each evening from five until seven. Their activities vary but their intimacy does not. Whatever else they do during the day is redeemed by this period. A man goes jogging regularly, through the countryside or a park, for forty minutes. The stress of running is sufficient to make it the only thing he thinks of. Yet immediately beneath his awareness of the present, in the familiar landmarks and the familiar stresses, is the sense that he has done this before and will do this again, that he characteristically wills to do it, that in doing it he enters and enlarges a part of himself which is unavailable to him at other times. Such periods unify us, concentrating our energy, judgment and emotion upon a single point. Conversely, they relieve us from all other considerations and so give us profound refreshment. They give us, if temporarily, ourselves. They are true acts of freedom, compared with which our normal miscellaneous diversions and indulgences of impulse are like the flutterings of moths.

VII.3 ⚘ UNSTRUCTURED TIME IS SELDOM FREE time; generally it is prevented, by distraction, interruption, indefinite dimensions and lack of regularity from being a suitable medium for the exercise of the will. In our normal lives, only the period between dinner and sleep approaches being a nest of time, a dimension of freedom. We can regularly depend upon enjoying these hours, and we tend to limit our range of activities in them. Their boundaries in time are definite and dependable and pleasant. During this period we seem to behave differently, not just because we are tired and satisfied, but also I think because we feel ourselves expanding within a quiet gulf of time, with no limits to overshadow, no spines to infringe upon our being. We are larger, lazier, more majestic; at once more like philosopher-kings and contented quadrupeds than we can possibly be during the day. To appreciate such periods is to wish to extend their freedoms into other parts of the day, other days of the year.

VII.4 ⚘ WHEN BUILDING A NEST OF TIME, BE certain of its dimensions. Its duration should not depend on something unpredictable — a homecoming, a phone call, or your own whim — for then its outer fringes, beginning and/or end, will be weakened by uncertainty. It should be long enough for the activity it includes, not so short as to be rushed or so long as to be oppressive. If possible it should look out, like a room in a country house, toward some pleasant prospect of future time — a meal, a meeting, a rest. Protect these periods also from within. A telephone or television set or radio, for example, can ruin time as thoroughly as a hole in the roof or a missing door can ruin interior space. A confused schedule, conflicting obligations or habitual distraction all crack the walls of time, leaving us defenseless against an infringing environment.

VII.5 ⚘ THE ESTABLISHMENT AND PRESERVATION of identity are, for most adults, less a process of discovery and assertion than a kind of recollection — if the word *recollection* be taken in its literal sense. We laze at the breakfast table on long

Saturday mornings, in the weekend haven from concerns which are at once narrow and dissipating; and slowly in the peace and quiet our individual characteristics regroup and reintegrate into coherent selves, friendships, marriages. These are important periods, as necessary to the total self as sleep is to the mind and body; they should be observed respectfully if not reverently. To be deprived of such free time is to be exiled from the self.

VII.6 🖎 WHEN, ON VACATION, WE LEAVE OUR home and work, we leave behind not only a particular place but also a particular sort of time. I mean this not only in the purely physical sense, in which no object or phenomenon is without its temporal coordinate, but also in the psychological sense that our habitual environment structures our sense of time and shapes the rhythm of our being. Familiar objects like the coffee maker, the dishwasher, the garbage pail, the dogfood dish and the mailbox subtly suggest their daily use — our daily debt to them — each time we glance at them. Larger areas of the house, even when they happen to be clean and well-maintained, suggest their perennial need for cleaning and maintenance. The very rooms, kitchen, bathroom, study, laundry, living room, bedroom, bespeak the times when we use them — times which, through the uniform demands of daily life, tend to grow into mechanical and uncompromising routine. The electric clock in the kitchen keeps a unique brand of local time, a time emanating not just from its own gears and current but from the whole house, beds, rugs, curtains, closets, pots and pans. And the time thus kept is no abstract measure, but rather the harmonic index of the health or cares or vanity of our inner lives. The sense of leaving this place, whether it is delight or sorrow, is also a sense of leaving time.

VII.7 🖎 THE SYMBOL OF PRIVATE HAPPINESS and triumphant humanity, from the days of Cicero down to the present, has been the summer home, with its implications of freedom, natural pleasures, conviviality and unencumbered time. This last element, the temporal dimension of happiness, is suggested not only by the habitual uses of the farm or cabin, but by its very dynamics of space. The "ideal" town or suburban living room, for example, in establishing its usually fallacious claims to personality, elegance and richness, becomes an enemy of comfort and a greedy monster for attention. Entering its confines we are instantly set on edge: we are embarrassed that our feet have trodden on vulgar earth; our palms sweat, and we rub them for grime; we lower our bottoms onto the petulantly fluffed cushions with a sense of sacrilege. Its demands are "Watch your step," "Leave me clean," and (in the literal words of a note to me from an absent landlord), "On second thought, you had better not use this chair at all." The living room of the self-respecting summer home, on the other hand, welcomes use, forgives misuse. Its typical artifacts — old chairs, damaged tables, dingy carpets, rat-eared mysteries — doggy yet godlike, oblige us in no way, suggesting diminished obeisance to the material world, and openness in time. The overall effect of such a residence is that of a sailboat in time, a banishment of psychological machinery and reversion to the broader and gentler motions of nature. So eased, we may regain touch with the childish and jubilant bases for involvement in life.

VII.8 ⚹ COMPETITIVE PLAY IS AN ESPECIALLY effective nest in time because its demands on our attention are so absolute. Many of us are likely to show more real seriousness at the chessboard or on the tennis court than, for periods of similar length, we show at our desks or at committee meetings. Why is this? While professional challenges are unremitting, diffuse and often miscellaneously distracting, the challenges of a game are autocratically structured, narrowly defined and limited by time. We obey the rules of a game with reverence and precision; for if we break those rules, the world degenerates into nonsense. Indeed, it is through this intense involvement that we realize one of the chief benefits of games: liberation from all our other concerns. In this sense, games are more relaxing than relaxation: for when we "relax," we often open ourselves up to a hive of worries and impulses, but when we concentrate on a game, or anything else that is meaningful and definite, our life temporarily becomes simple and pure. To

say that a psychologically healthy person "sees little distinction between work and play" is partly to miss the point, unless we add
that his attitude toward both work and play, though not solemn or
vain, is lively and intent.

VII.9 ✍ Chess, which exists predominantly
in two dimensions, is one of the world's most difficult games.
Three-dimensional chess is an invitation to insanity. But human relationships, even of the simplest order, are like a kind of four-
dimensional chess, a game whose pieces and positions change subtly
and inexorably *between* moves, whose players stare dumbly while
their powerful positions deteriorate into hopeless predicaments and
while improbable combinations suddenly become inevitable. To
make matters worse, some games are open to any number of players, and all sides are expected to win.

VII.10 ✍ Winning tennis players are
characteristically alert to the importance of aftermaths: the points
or games immediately following intense and hotly-contested moments of play. Both the winner and the loser of these violent flurries
tend naturally to be weak in the aftermath: the winner, because his
temporary glory seduces him into relaxing, and the loser, whose
frustration may induce careless errors or cause him to try too hard.
One way or another, these aftermath points and games are likely to
be lost on errors; and therefore the wise player approaches them
conservatively and with full concentration. Something like this
holds true in other forms of experience as well. In our generally
fragmentary perception of time, our plebeian fascination with goals
and ends, we often mistake the climax of an experience for its completion, responding dully and coldly to the period which follows.
We fail to cast a glance backwards, to complete the event with an
awareness of its passing. We leave time's dirty dishes in the sink.
This failure not only causes errors, poor memory and periods of
unredeemed oblivion; it also contributes to a sense of time in which
nothing is continuous, nothing complete.

VII.II ⚸ OUR CONCEPTION OF PSYCHOLOGY, LIKE many of our other most important notions, is spatial in character. We see the mind as an onionlike layering of conscious and unconscious processes which exist continuously and simultaneously. But temporality should not be excluded from this image; for though we may be multileveled, we are also *modal*, in the sense that at any given time only one level of our complexity is normally available to us. The difference between our waking and dreaming selves is a classic example of this modality; other disparities can be found between our behavior at work and at home, with our own sex and with the opposite sex, with others and by ourselves. Anger, desire, fear and other emotions are also capable of establishing modal identities — complete if temporary patterns of awareness and action. Many of these modes have urgent subconscious roots and, while they hold sway, dominate and define our character. From this springs one of the chief characteristics of individual behavior: that, caught in a given mode, we are isolated from all other modes, unable to gain perspective or call our full resources into play. This fact, coupled with our often very sudden shifts in mode and the general difficulty of remembering one mode from the vantage point of another, contributes much to the overall complexity of human behavior and the defects of consistency, improvement and self-knowledge which bother all of us. We are different people, strangers to ourselves, as givers and receivers, as theoreticians and tacticians, as private versus public beings. We are different as hosts from what we are as guests, as lovers from what we are as friends, as drivers from what we are as pedestrians, as judges from what we are as pleaders. And these distinctions, if radical and specific enough, not only cause confusion but become the natural raw material of hypocrisy. True self-knowledge, available to most of us only at exceptional moments and for longer periods only to exceptional individuals, is not just a depth of perception, then, but also a kind of simultaneity, a comprehensive grasp, sympathetic but not subjugated, of several temporal modes at once.

VII.12 ⚸ DURING THE PAST TWO DECADES A LARGE number of psychologists have variously promoted the idea of enhanced expressiveness. It has been argued that we must express our anger and our affection, our urge for dominance or our feeling of impotence; that females should express their femaleness, males their maleness, races their ethnicity; that in general the mind should reform itself into a kind of liberal democracy whose psychological citizens are accorded eminence for their loudness as well as their eloquence; that a conglomeration of "inner" impulses, simplified under the popular title of "It," be allowed like some hidden organ, phallic but fatigued, to "all hang out." Recently (and predictably) a countercurrent has welled up, attacking enhanced expressiveness as a kind of "Me-ism" and condemning its popular formulations as euphemistic trappings for subjectivity and selfishness. There is much in what these debunkers say; but we should beware lest they in their enthusiasm project us back toward the opaqueness and taciturnity of an earlier generation. Indeed, the problem with both sides is that they interpret the word *expressiveness* rather simplistically. Expressiveness, most fully conceived, is revealed identity, identity in action. Not only our emotions, therefore, but also our conscious control over those emotions, must be termed *self-expression*. Emotions may be unimpeachable marks of identity, but will and control are what integrate and define identity and save it from the entropy of warring impulsive forces. By controlling ourselves we express our humanness, both particular and general: we define self from the raw components of self; and we adopt a uniquely human attitude toward time in consciously sacrificing some present desire in favor of the continuum. We can also know our own emotions better, and enjoy them more, if we allow them to define themselves in a context of control.

VII.13 ⚹ INDIVIDUALS WHO HAVE, FROM ONE cause or another, flirted with genuine self-knowledge, are aware of the curious impulse to become their own opposites. The gentle wish to be bold, the mercurial patient, the industrious lazy, the temperate passionate. Conscious of our own psychological convexities and concavities, we wish to turn ourselves inside out, to taste fresh being at the alien polarity. And those who one way or another achieve these reversals, expecting strange new experiences, are often surprised by the native and intimate familiarity of the forms they have assumed.

VII.14 ✍ LEARN YOUR OWN FAULTS AND VICES; but do not assume that all of them should be eradicated. Sometimes, like beasts serving a greater master, they provide necessary balance and thus deserve indulgence; sometimes they are the indivisible shadows of virtues themselves.

VII.15 ✍ BECAUSE TIME IS CONTINUOUS AND homogeneous, every action or emotion has meaning and value of its own, irrespective of cause, purpose or result. Love, admiration and reverence have positive meaning, even when it turns out that their object does not deserve them. Care, patience and courage have positive meaning, even when the project fails. Conversely anger, scorn and disgust, no matter how justifiable, lower us, make us less; and boredom is not only a judgment about experience but a sin against ourselves. Thus we must live the present not only in context but out of context, see it not only as a link in a chain but as a kind of poetic essence, impermanent and absolute. Affirming what must be affirmed, denying what must be denied, we should nonetheless be careful lest our denials outnumber our affirmations, lest our lives degenerate into rear-guard actions against grossness and nastiness. For the emotions and postures of the present, like elemental forms, retain their identity no matter how they are compounded.

VII.16 ✍ THE MIND PROJECTS ITS JOYS AND WOES so powerfully onto the face of time that changes in mood can all but create new temporal worlds. The negative or painful emotions — guilt, anger, envy, greed, etc. — usually involve a fragmentation of time, a sense of isolation in the present or fixation on some aspect of the past or future. The sunny emotions — admiration, generosity, love, courage, etc. — foster a sense of continuity, of time extended and shared. Calm people swim freely into the future and speak of it as if it were part of them. But those who are hopeless for reasons of age or grief or illness barely use the future tense at all; and for frightened people the future can shrink to almost nothing, can seem like the rippled surface of water between them and some menacing promontory. Opportunists live in a tiny

glimmer of the present, intent like small predators on the next mor-
sel or trap. Win or lose, time is for them a straitened and barren
dimension. But for happy people, at the opposite extreme, the present is so voluminous, so inclusive of the full self and so indivisibly
coherent with past and future, that time in the usual sense does not
pass for them at all. They are at one with the dynamics of nature:
time's motion is implicit in their own.

VII.17 ✒ OUR BLINDNESS TO TIME IS
particularly severe with regard to its middle distances, its weeks
and months. While we are perfectly well aware that a day has gone
nicely or badly, or that a year has been happy or indifferent or
rough, we seldom keep regular track of the components of basic
change or stasis, the choices or evasions which, countlessly and automatically repeated, drive us along one line or another. We see
the end results — that we have fallen out of touch with our family,
that we have exhausted ourselves yet achieved little, or that, like
poor Hamlet, we have grown "fat, and out of breath," and like
drunken drivers we veer to avert disaster; but we habitually ignore
the raw materials of these phenomena, the mechanisms of choice
which, like the ceaseless erosion of channels, confirm themselves
into blind habit. In order to reassert control over these mechanisms, we must first become aware of them. But they are difficult
to evaluate in isolation. Many of them consist in evasion rather
than action and hence are as though invisible. Others, like all individual sins and failings, carry their own assortments of credible
excuses. The best we can do, I think, is not to pick nits but rather
to consult broader purposes, taking time off every few days to review our position in life, evaluating the present in terms of past and
future, memories and plans, and determining the ways in which recent and present choices may suggest larger patterns. In so doing,
we rise temporarily above the ordinary flow of time and reacquaint
ourselves with the larger pattern of forces which is our enduring
identity.

VII.18 FROM A MODERN BOOK-JACKET:

> Such civilized writing and observation are rare in the United States nowadays, and on its merits M—— is pretty certainly the best contemporary chronicle, so far, of its place and period.

A remarkable utterance from a judge of "civilized writing." After unaccountably putting "writing" before "observation" and after leaving no doubt that it is "on its merits" that the book is to be praised, the reviewer dishes up an impressive chronological redundancy: "contemporary chronicle . . . of its place and period" buttressed by the wholly absurd "so far." Such errors and excesses are by no means uncommon in writing and speech. They point to our general fear of being set adrift in time, our need to establish context and position in a dimension which torments us with formlessness and confusion. They remind me of an excellent story ("The Outstation") by W. Somerset Maugham, in which an English colonial official, isolated in a remote Eastern wilderness, receives, several months late, large bundles of the London *Times*. He religiously avoids consulting the latest one first, but rather stacks them in chronological order, reading but one each day until he reaches the bottom of the pile. His only English associate thinks him a fool. But if so, his folly is universal, his practice simply a more dramatic rendering of our often unfulfilled need to locate ourselves in a reasonable context of time.

VII.19 WE ARE TOLD THAT THE INDIVIDUAL lives to the beat of a number of inner clocks ("biorhythms") which move at different speeds. Whether or not this is true (at present it is both an hypothesis and a fad), we do seem to possess a number of psychological clocks – awarenesses of various aspects of experience – which simultaneously and independently beat at different speeds. For example, sitting distractedly at my desk, I can consult my watch three times in five minutes: once to see whether the mail has come (business time), once to find out how many hours of writing I have left (creative time) and once to ascertain the nearness of lunch (belly time). One sort of time may pass quickly for me while another passes quite slowly; and I may simultaneously try to extenuate one cycle while wishing that another will slow up. On a broad scale, these distinctions in pace are more striking. Two events from the same time in the past can seem, respectively, recent and ancient. I look back sixteen days. The great event of that day — a young couple's arrival from the East to stay with us and help out by babysitting — seems new and fresh; but what I wrote that day, obscured by sixteen days of intervening work and washed out by sixteen nights of oblivion, looks strange and old.

VII.20 🖎 EVERY TIME WE POSTPONE SOME necessary event — whether we put off doing the dinner dishes till morning or defer an operation or some difficult labor or study — we do so with the implication that present time is more important than future time (for if we wished the future to be as free and comfortable as we wish the present to be, we would perform necessary actions as soon as they prove themselves necessary). There is nothing wrong with this, as long as we know what we are doing, and as long as the present indeed holds some opportunity more important than the task we delay. But very often our decision to delay is less a free choice than a semiconscious mechanism — a conspiracy between our reasoning awareness and our native dislike of pain. The result of this conspiracy is a disconcerting contradiction of will; for when we delay something, we simultaneously admit its necessity and refuse to do it. Seen more extensively, habitual delays can clutter our lives, leave us in the annoying position of always having to do yesterday's chores. Disrespect for the future is a subtly poisonous disrespect for self, and forces us, paradoxically enough, to live in the past.

VII.21 🖎 MINOR DISAGREEMENTS ABOUT projected activities are usually dominated by people who have planned for these activities in advance. It is as though they gained power and momentum by projecting their wills forward in time.

VII.22 🖎 PLANS MADE SWIFTLY AND INTUITIVELY are likely to have flaws. Plans made carefully and comprehensively are sure to.

VII.23 🖎 IN THE LANDSCAPE OF TIME, THERE ARE few locations less comfortable than that of one who waits for some person or event to arrive at some unknown moment in the future. As such we are hooked onto the future and dangle helplessly on lines of doubt, anxiety or expectation. The best way to wait is *not* to wait: to retire into what Montaigne calls, psychologically, the "back-shop"; to drift fully into our own concerns and away from external tyrannies. For such periods, the following antidotes to distraction may be of some use:

1. Exercise your memory, running through recent experiences, new acquaintances, current events, the substance of books, etc.
2. Review your short-term and long-term goals.
3. Review your recent and current impressions, verbalizing them in your mind or on paper.
4. List your present worries, desires and other concerns, and set them within a larger temporal context.
5. Think about some important errors you have made, or some things you have done well. Try to analyze the causes, principles and psychological tonalities that have gone into each.
6. Withdraw yourself from the situation you are in, and imagine the life around you as it would be without you.
7. If there are strangers around you (in a doctor's office, a bus station, etc.) put yourself in the place of one of them; imagine his or her feelings, his or her day.
8. Reconstruct as fully as possible some bygone house, room, character or event.
9. Try to remember what, at some point in the past, you expected this period to be like.

VII.24 🖎 YOU MAY CURE YOURSELF OF A depression by forcing yourself to perform, in rapid order and with excruciating concentration, half a dozen or so unpleasant chores,

especially if they have long been postponed. This is a kind of ho-
meopathic purgative, a treatment of like with like.

VII.25 ✑ IF YOU ARE FEARFUL OF SOME EVENT IN
the future, and all reasonable efforts to calm your fear have failed,
try worrying about it as intensely, lengthily and specifically as possible. The exhausting experience of worry, which is a kind of pre-
living of events, may well defuse your anxiety when the event
actually occurs. In the same sense, conscious worry encourages us
to formulate solutions to the problems we will be facing. At any
rate, do not try to repress or stifle your fear of what is to come.
This is a sure path to anxiety in action.

VII.26 ✑ FOR A WHILE NOW I HAVE KEPT, ALONG
with our more traditional timepieces, a digital watch which shows
hours, minutes and seconds in illuminated Arabic numerals. Such
watches, my wife remarks, give their wearers a wholly different
idea of time. Looking at them we see a particular time, divorced
from its context in the broader picture of the day. The round faces
of the older watches and clocks speak to us not only of the present
but also of the past and the future — when we woke, when we will
work or play or rest, where we have been, where we wish to be or
must be. Intricately and persistently they remind us of our existence in a continuum, which includes not only the social and natural world but also our own extending identity in time. The new
watches, like many other modern and businesslike things, ignore
such frivolities, demarcating only that particular island of time on
which we happen to be stranded.

VII.27 ✑ THE PROCESS OF ABSTRACTION—
by which we denote classes of phenomena by means of their shared
characteristics — is at the root of language and systematic thought.
Plato defined philosophy itself as the progressive ascent of increas-

ingly elevated levels of abstraction.* An analogous, though predominantly nonintellectual, form of abstraction seems to occur in the emotional development of a child. A boy's first love object is his mother; his first material goals are the possessions of father and/or older siblings; his first ambition is the authority and privileges of the older males. The root of all his later love and yearning will be the love and yearning for these early things. As such things are necessarily unattainable by him as an individual, he is led to seek attainable things which resemble them. With this step, his conscious will and visceral inclination have abstracted themselves from the particular and reached the first level of private freedom. With fortunate individuals, this development continues. The adolescent begins to realize that his own unique character and altered circumstances suggest goals which are qualitatively distinct from the primal models. The mature individual may reach a further level of abstraction, realizing that particular goals are not desirable in themselves, but rather because they possess innately desirable characteristics. He will be, to some extent at least, free from the anxious and potentially self-destructive yearning for particulars, and open to the qualitative understanding which may in time set him above the marketplace of ordinary seekers.

VII.28 ✄ WE ARE WISTFUL ABOUT THE GOLDEN days of the past and dream of a distant future unclouded by necessity. But I suspect that if our inner souls were asked what in life they really missed, the answer would be primal danger and stress.

VII.29 ✄ DO NOT BE IMPATIENT ABOUT THE future when you know that it contains good things. Instead, enjoy these as future things, as often and lingeringly as possible. Events can be enjoyed in all three dimensions of time: as future, present and past. Impatience robs you of the first of these three enjoyments; and this is the sadder because the enjoyment of the future is by no means the least extensive of the three and contains quali-

---

* *Symposium*, 210–212.

ties — a simplicity and a pure willingness — possessed by neither of the others.

VII.30 ⚹ YOU MAY EXPECT MUCH FROM LIFE, in the way of development and improvement; but never expect to transcend or escape the common weaknesses of humanity. If you do not succeed, you will pine for success; if you are successful, you will regret what you gave up in order to succeed. You will envy those above you and, should you reach the top, you will fear those climbing up to take your place. You will worry about your children and complain about their errors, even if they are doing quite well. You will be stung by criticism or neglect even when it comes from fools. You will worry about money, no matter how much you have. Should you become a great personage, you will nonetheless drop names like a sycophant. You will feel pain and shame at signs of age and yet, to your dying day, make mouths in your mirror. And if you manage, with great effort, to avoid or subdue one of these vices, you will be deucedly proud of yourself. For time, which can extend and magnify you, cannot liberate you from the confines of your skin or alter nature from its enduring shape.

VIII ⚘ GROWTH
AND AGE ⚘ ⚘

VIII.1 ⚘ THE CHILD OF TWO OR THREE, WHO knows neither past nor future, sees, knows, becomes the present more than we can understand or remember. For him space and temporality are limitless, and each distinct experience, whether or not he has had it before, adds another chapter to an unending sequence of newness. He concentrates better than we do; and his concentration knows no purpose and needs none because, unlike us, he is still sensible to the animate magic of the physical world. To say that he has no sense of time is fatuous, for his sense of the present is so lordly and encompassing — like some vast sunny chamber or garden with room for innumerable pleasures and occupations — that he is beyond time as we know it, closer to St. Augustine's conception of a timeless God. As he is still a stranger to memory, conscience, aim and ambition, his inner time is not limited by these factors, and so may expand to identify itself with his external environment. Perhaps, with our assistance, he will be able to take traces of this dignity and serenity into later life. We should not interrupt him when he is happy or entertain him in such a way that his attention will be divided.

VIII.2 ⚘ THE ACT OF CONCENTRATING ON A GIVEN subject is, conversely, the act of temporarily forgetting everything else. This is one reason why, in most cases, highly successful people seem to be possessed of great calm and impressive reserves of energy. Capable of intense concentration on basic questions, they are not worn down by superficial difficulties, distracting side issues or the enervating friction of a divided mind. Professionally hard at work, they are psychologically on vacation: this is one case where conventional achievement is completely in accord with mental and physical health. Speaking more generally, concentration is the forgotten component of intelligence, the virtue whose absence, more than anything else, characterizes the weakness of modern education. Our American IQ tests, in which a student's total ability is estimated from his success or failure in answering a long series of distinct and specific questions, is an example of our failure to understand the power of concentration or to respect the patience, humility and grandness of vision it requires. The results of this failure, in large part, are hundreds of thousands of young people who are sensitive but dissatisfied and disoriented, hundreds of thousands of mature intellectuals who are devastatingly bright on specific questions but devastatedly impotent in terms of larger projects.

VIII.3 ✍ ONE OF THE COMMONEST FALLACIES of child-rearing is that babies have characteristic likes and dislikes, abilities and defects, which may be ascertained from repeated instances and will hold true thereafter. Parents with the faith and tenacity to keep trying soon realize that this is nonsense. Babies and tiny children are all will; but theirs is fluid will, power without rigidity. They are also subject to an evolution of awareness so constant and profound that the "same" object or experience can, over the course of a few weeks, appear to them as a number of wholly different things. The fact that a given course of action has ten times failed to teach or satisfy a child is absolutely no proof that the same course will not succeed the next time round; and children who have seemed chronically defective in a given area will often develop sudden and titanic prowess in that area. To see children as having ingrained characteristics is to endow them, quite mistakenly, with adult weaknesses; when we do so, we prematurely bestow these weaknesses upon them. Instead we must be optimistic, flexible and relentless.

VIII.4 ✍ OBEDIENCE IS THE NECESSARY CONTEXT for education and indeed for survival; moreover, it is the primal matter or substructure of what will later be self-control. But teaching obedience is difficult, particularly because it must occur during the same period when the child is discovering his own individual will. With this difficulty in mind, it is expedient to educate a child in obedience as much as possible through positive rather than negative commands or suggestions. When we tell a child to do something, we ask him to assert his will. On the other hand, when we tell him not to do something, we contradict his will as actually or potentially asserted. The positive thus carries more permanent weight than the negative; and if we gain a child's respect through positive directives, he will be more likely to obey such negative directives as must also be given. Here, as in most other interpersonal relationships, the primogeniture of will operates strongly: the earlier asserter has a subtle but undeniable advantage and can, if perceptive, determine the course of the action. But this sort of beforehandedness is, I repeat, not easy for parents to achieve. Our children's wills, because they are so intensely vivid and resilient, project them ahead of us in time, leaving us helplessly to condemn or commend their *faits accomplis*.

VIII.5 ✍ THE TEACHER-STUDENT RELATIONSHIP, largely devoid of self-interest and rich in psychological power, is perhaps the most beautiful and effective interaction which civilization affords. No culture I know of has ever fully used the power of this relationship, and indeed most cultures reserve for the young a privilege which people of all ages and in all positions should share.

VIII.6 ✍ WE GENERALLY FEEL THAT WE MUST choose between coddling and suppressing teenagers, when instead our proper function is to challenge them, through demand, ridicule, frustration, cajolement, domination, example and enchantment. We must never be hesitant about correcting them and indeed embarrassing them in the process. Loss, failure and chagrin are as important to proper education as pain is to the health of the body.

Realizing error is a spur to careful and accurate performance. More profoundly, the repeated small disgraces and humiliations of learning encourage students to discard the meaner aspects of identity — vanity, defensiveness, affectation and the eagerness for petty victories — which would otherwise inhibit them from real appreciation and achievement. Delight and dignity lie behind this wall of pain. Educators who revere this process realize that they cannot achieve it if they remain "on easy and familiar terms" with their students. They are aware that the teacher, whose work is a high form of love, cannot seek to be loved in return.

VIII.7 ✒ MANY MODERN TEACHERS AND theorists of education believe in making learning "fun" — making its early stages gamelike and pleasant rather than arduous. This method is natural and effective with small children, but less so in high school and college, where it generally results in a dilution of learning and a depreciation of its excitement and dignity. The apologists for this theory tend to forget that the process of learning is itself innately pleasurable and that this true pleasure is likely to be hidden or distempered if we present it with the dishonesty of a publicist. A more dynamic method is preferable — one in which a study, initially described as almost mysteriously difficult, becomes, as the students invade it, an increasingly delightful exploration. This latter method implies a greater respect for students and is also closer to nature, for in nature we learn by struggle as well as by play.

VIII.8 ✒ AN ORDINARY TEACHER WEIGHS AND bags ideas like potatoes; a skilled teacher makes them open up like flowers from a bud.

VIII.9 ✒ THE STATE OF MODERN HIGHER education resembles that of an oak tree in a drought. Most oaks will survive one dry season, but not two in a row. Higher education is now entering its second season of drought: a generation in which the untaught will be taught by the untaught.

VIII.10 ✒ EVERY TEACHER, WHETHER HE KNOWS it or not, teaches three things at once: the subject under investigation, the art of investigation and the art of teaching. The two latter teachings, which concern method rather than matter, are more subtle, more lasting and more important. We teach them by patient and unadvertised repetition, showing through time how the same method works in a variety of cases. Only through this combination of coherence and variety can the student grasp the nature of method — abstract it and see it as something distinct from the specific subject matter and the specific character of the teacher. More advanced students should be shown how a variety of methods can be applied to the same subject. Both these levels of teaching are like perambulations, walkings around an object in an effort to comprehend its dimensions and form. In the first case, we walk around method itself; in the second, we walk around a subject. In a third and still higher form of learning, we seek a master method, discovering through repetition and abstraction what all valid methods have in common.

VIII.11 ✒ FEW FALLACIES ARE MORE DANGEROUS or easier to fall into than that by which, having read a given book, we assume that we will continue to know its contents permanently or, having mastered a discipline in the past, we assume that we control it in the present. Philosophically speaking, "to learn" is a verb with no legitimate past tense.

VIII.12 ✒ SINCE THE TRUTH IS SO OFTEN the opposite of what most people believe, and since most beliefs are not abandoned without a fight, the good lecture must have not only a plan but a strategy. It should initially touch on established belief and, if possible, evoke a statement or statements of such belief from its audience. It should then complicate this belief as something dependent upon prejudice, poor methodology or outright paradox. It should turn with a violent grace on the crisis between opinion and truth.

VIII.13 ✍ WE TEND TO CELEBRATE IN OURSELVES and others, under the general rubric of "maturity," an assortment of qualities whose common denominator is sedateness: moderation, circumspection, ironic distance, meticulousness, discretion and "perspective"; and we praise these qualities highly when they occur precociously in the young. Yet great achievers, whom we rightly exalt, seem to be characterized by qualities almost the opposite of these and indeed suggestive of extreme youth: boldness, decisiveness, openness to emotion, rebelliousness and enthusiasm. Why are we enemies of greatness? We wish to protect society. We inculcate virtues which are protective, which guard gains and minimize losses, which ensure us from disaster, confusion and shame. Conversely, therefore, we discourage virtues which are exploratory and inquisitive; even though it is these latter virtues which, at some point in the past, forged our present security out of conflict and danger. And in so doing we verge on one of the major sins against time: that miserly caution, that scorn of promise which, instead of protecting us, snags us destructively against the general flow. Our motives are debatable. Perhaps we wish to protect the young. Perhaps we reason from our own personal failures, or are so chronologically subjective as to have forgotten that we once were, in critically important ways, better than we are now. Or perhaps, through fear and envy of the young, we wish to prevent them from getting what we think we have, or achieving where we tried and failed.

VIII.14 ✍ THE MOCKERY OF ESTABLISHED VALUE and the rebellion against it are essential experiences of youth. In this high form of play, we learn our weaknesses through initiatives of omnipotence, our communality through assertions of uniqueness, our loneliness through charades of independence. We may at last emerge as beings capable of changing or renewing the system; but this is much more likely if the system has, from the beginning, made its strengths plain and clear to us. Autocratic societies, which stifle the young and proclaim value as law, voluntarily perpetuate their own weakness through the generations. Liberal democracies, whose intellectuals have evolved "beyond" moral value and hence assert nothing, do not do much better; for they give their young little to fight for, and nothing to rebel against. Good societies make demands on their young, yet allow them freedom for frivolity; they advertise their form yet show respect for chaos.

VIII.15 ✍ THE ACCUSATION THAT CONTEMPORARY society is afflicted with a "cult of youth" is only partly true. If we had a genuine cult of youth, we would love and fawn over the young and give much thought to their education, improvement and delight. What we see today is more a middle-aged usurpation of youth, an attempt by the middle-aged to commandeer, through nostalgia fads, freakish styles, hairblowers, skin-oils and inarticulate slang, the supposedly happy condition of youth. And while we spend millions for blue jeans redesigned to accommodate our sagging nates, real attention to the young is funded on a level with such other social services as corrections, sanitation and pest control; and the young spend their years of pristine felicity in cheap schools, taught by belittled drudges and endeavoring, with every means at their disposal, to perfect the vices of maturity.

VIII.16 ✍ AS WE GROW OLDER, OUR YOUTH silently expands in time, while old age conversely contracts. At twenty-two, having graduated from college, I considered my youth at an end, forgetting that I had come to a similar conclusion on leaving high school at eighteen. Now in my forties, I consider my life up to age thirty-three a kind of twilight adolescence, thirty-three through thirty-six as *Lehrjahre*, and thirty-seven on as young manhood. Old age, which once for me included the late thirties, has now accordingly scuttled back into the underbrush beyond age sixty-five. I expect that this process will continue, at least in a kind of parabolic curve, through my whole life. At fifty I will probably look back at forty, with indulgence born perhaps of envy, as unpracticed and supple greenness. I and others like me live in a kind of eternal middle age, and no wonder; for no matter where we are in age, we are always in the middle of time, and must weigh our future equally with our past.

VIII.17   THE IDEA OF MY OWN ADVANCING AGE has never particularly bothered me, perhaps because my youthful years were much less enjoyable than the time I have now. But to-day, prompted by some new ache or wrinkle, my mind glanced onto the subject, and I was briefly invaded by a curious feeling. It was the same sort of mood that is cultivated by writers of thrillers, experienced by heroes who, early in the story, are knocked out or drugged, and awake to find themselves in wholly unfamiliar places, damp moldering cellars or drab rooms whose barred windows look out on alien courtyards, far from where the heroes' friends or colleagues expect them to be, far from where they or anyone would want to be. They feel dismay, confusion and impotent anger, and these were what I momentarily felt; but in my case the feeling did not concern place but rather time. I felt stranded in my forties, a young spirit in a withering body. For a few instants I refused to acknowledge my body as my own, denied the connection between awareness and the protoplasm from which it springs. It was not until later that I realized that this refusal, this anger, was the real crux of aging: that the pain of growing old lies specifically in the fact that part of us does not grow old.

VIII.18   HAVING CHILDREN TRANSFIGURES psychological time in two ways. First, the proliferation of important events (that is, experiencing your child's/or children's life as well as your own) speeds up time, much the same way a proliferation of notes speeds up music. Parents become multiple identities, caught willy-nilly in multiple time frames; the graceful marriage waltz becomes a kind of breathless communal jig. Second, the fact of parenthood forces us to project our own being far forward into time and endows the newly-discovered future with unaccustomed drama. I will be sixty, for example, when my older son graduates from college, sixty-three when my younger son graduates. Financially, this is well and good: should I still be employed as a professor, my salary will be near its peak; and under present law, I will not have to retire until my younger son is through graduate school or into a career. Emotionally, however, things look less good. I will be seventy, entering the decades of luck, before I can reasonably expect grandchildren. I will be extremely fortunate (age seventy-eight) to see, as my father has seen at a much younger age, a son reach forty. In all probability, I will not live to see my children attain professional maturity; and I must confess that this grieves me. These are all simple facts I could have and probably did think about during the nine married years when, for a number of reasons, my wife and I delayed having children. But in those earlier thoughts I had not had the transfiguring experience of loving children and of feeling my own future expand and stretch with theirs.

VIII.19 ✍ SOME POLITICAL SPOKESMEN CLAIM that the Western world is dominated by a white minority; others, that the world is run by a conspiracy of males. Both claims are accurate, but this is not the half of it. The world is, in fact, a monopoly of white middle-aged men, a closed shop of paunches, cranky prostates and bloodshot eyes. By some miraculous coincidence of good public relations and global stupidity, the dominance of this chronological cabal has up to now passed largely unnoticed. How did they seize power? To understand is to accord them grudging respect. They were, originally, thrown into the job by circumstance, the young being silly, the old weak. Their characteristic accomplishments and psychological attributes (they are, for example, toilet-trained, careful at streetcorners and slow to take offense) accord fairly well with the maintenance of political order. We should not be outraged so much by the fact that the middle-aged created civilization *by* themselves but rather by the extent to which they have created it *for* themselves — the extent to which the problems and eccentricities of culture comport with a middle-aged image. We should question tax laws which reward caution and punish enterprise, institutional structures which educate new-comers in the art of the *status quo* while leaving them ignorant of basic principles. And we should question, also, the smaller de-tails: why great department stores and office buildings have so few places where tired people can sit and rest; why public restrooms, designed and sanitized by the utilitarian wisdom of the ages, lack toilet seats scaled to the million emergencies of smaller bottoms.

VIII.20 ✍ WISDOM, WHICH IS GIVEN TO FEW people young or old, is mistakenly supposed to be the property of the old, and hence despised by all. Indeed the very word, which once denoted profound and comprehensive intelligence, has shrunk into a kind of defensive prudence, an attribute shared by watchful pedestrians, cautious investors and tourists who do not forget to bring along their pills. Our noblest horse now pulls a manure wagon; our best idea, once the goal of every enlightened life, is now forgotten, and its verbal symbol attached to mean concerns. Yet the word *wisdom* retains some value; for in its pathetic decline we may read the Lilliputian vanity of the modern spirit.

VIII.21 ✍ TWO NIGHTS AGO I SAT WITH MY WIFE and her mother in a lamp-lit room. My mother-in-law, a woman of seventy whose beauty increases with age, spoke of a memoir she is writing about her father, who died almost forty years ago and whose name is shared by our older son. The conversation in the amber light, with its relaxed, somewhat fatigued composure, its frequent silences and its emphasis, both heard and seen, on large gaps of age, seemed like something snatched out of time, a paint-ing or photograph, a frame of stillness removed from the con-tinuum which had created the evening and would erase it. My wife and I, her mother and the ancestors and children we spoke of, seemed less like absolute individuals than like moments of hu-manity, attributes and respects of a longer identity, against whose grandness we had the wistful and pathetic detail of miniatures.

VIII.22 ✍   NOTHING IS SO SUBTLE, SO ELEGANTLY patient, as the encroachment upon us of age. It is a net woven around and through us, which insists, not in sudden tension or in the strength of any single filament, but rather in the gentle tightening, now of one side, now of another. A beauty of twenty-eight, examining her eyes in the mirror for pouches or hen's feet, smiles when she finds none; not noticing the elusive shadow, the delicate hollowing above her upper eyelids, which will mark her as a woman in her thirties, or seeing that her own intense scrutiny is deepening the lines of care between her upper lip and cheeks. A man of forty-five weighs himself regularly and increases his jogging distances; yet slimness, wind and muscle will not prevent the onset of the wooden posture and grooved mannerisms of middle age. And much subtler still is the internal advance of age, the silent ebbing of aspiration, the swell of weariness, the secret channels through which our spirits run from openness to assertiveness, from assertiveness to defensiveness, from defensiveness to scorn and the deadly safety of the closed mind.

VIII.23 ✍   TWO QUICK AND EASY WAYS OF growing old are (1) to resist change obstinately and (2) to worship it abjectly. In the first case, we are caught like snags in a river, worn down and bleached by the flow of experience. In the second, we are fatigued and wrinkled by innumerable reorchestrations to circumstance. Those who remain fresh and vital, as though they floated in time, are people who understand permanence as a balance of dynamics rather than a constitution of detail, who retain the youthful mechanism of converting change into growth. These people greet change with a kind of returning wonderment, not only because each change suggests, in one way or another, a renewal of their world, but also because in the very rhythm of change they find something natively familiar, some inexpressible reminder of the deepest attributes of self.

VIII.24 ✍   READING *King Lear*, I AM REMINDED how very few tragedies have heroes or heroines who are old.

Tragedy is by nature a conflict of strength against strength, of grand social or natural forces overcoming monumental assertions of individual will; and old age of itself does not suggest the vigor necessary for such massive conflict. Shakespeare solves this problem by giving his hero a fund of animal energy which spends itself explosively, as though Lear were exhausting a decade's strength in a month's crisis. And by so succeeding, Shakespeare calls our attention to another tragedy, subtle and universal, which is old age itself — where the conflict between vital will and decaying nature is fought in each of us, silently and solitarily, but often with a cumulative intensity equal to anything we see on the stage. Old age need not be the tragedy of life; but at least it is the tragic test of life, the conflict in which the unquenchable spirit must face pain and death without vigor of flesh, tribal support or the hope of future joys on earth.

VIII.25   COMMONLY OLD AGE BRINGS ON retirement from work; but in many cases it is truer to say that retirement brings on old age. The mind, like any other organ, retains and renews its strength only through exercise. In active life, whatever its negative stresses and trials, this exercise is emotional as well as rational, creative as well as defensive. The demands of communal effort constitute an irreplaceable exercise of mind, as does the state of being responsible or the state of being needed, no matter what the responsibility or the need. In retirement we lose these healthy activities, and the freedom we gain is often a poor exchange for the enervating vacuum of challenge, the dry rot of immobility which leaves us, month by month, less supple, less responsive and less vigorous. And even worse than this, to the extent that in active life we have established our own identity as social beings, we become in retirement less and less ourselves.

VIII.26   WE HAVE NUMEROUS EXAMPLES OF artists (Monet, Picasso, Chagall) and musicians (Stravinsky, Casals, Toscanini) who retained fabulous energy and buoyancy through old age. Perhaps this is because they were constantly beginning new projects. They maintained themselves because they characteristically stretched beyond themselves; they flourished because their minds and bodies unstintingly stretched forward into time. This evergreen awareness can be found in much simpler and less illustrious lives; but in these, being so alien to common sense and common knowledge, it is seldom adequately appreciated. When we hear of old people learning new languages, studying history or taking up some hobby from scratch, we often wonder how they can delude themselves into such fruitless enterprise. We should wonder instead what mysterious process enabled them to attain, at this or any age, such remarkable health of mind.

VIII.27 ✒ APPARENTLY ONE OF THE STEPS OF aging and dying is the rejection of the future. When we are old we do few things for the first time, many for the last time. We stop projecting our identities forward through the years and think more in terms of months. Planning anything becomes a form of bravado. And there must arise the awful temptation, cognate with despair, to damn the future altogether, expunge the future tense from our vocabularies, and stand with our backs to the blank wall of death. This act is suicidal, for the death of the future is the death of joy, almost of soul. We can avoid it, as I have said earlier, by concerning ourselves regularly and vigorously with new beginnings. And we can attempt the even more profound renewal, available I think only to the old, of partially shedding our individual selves and participating in a grander social and biological identity.

VIII.28 ✒ PEOPLE COMMONLY ASSUME that each passing second brings them closer to death; but this is largely and dangerously fallacious. The second in which a drowning man grabs hold of a life preserver or a starving man is offered a bowl of soup does not bring either closer to death but, rather, sharply away from it. People who undergo healthy conversions of habit cut abruptly away from death; wholesome exercise, from a physiological point of view, is not necessarily motion toward death at all. To say that such actions or activities merely delay death

is a kind of sophistry; for since death is, in physical terms, a negative state, it is much more pertinent and correct to say that they
prolong and increase life. Indeed, time has much less to do with
death — for death is, as a cessation of motion, also a cessation of
time — than it has to do with life, its most complex embodiment.
Thinking that time brings death is less a workable assumption than
a moral evasion, an example of our chronic tendency to ascribe our
woes and weaknesses to external circumstance rather than to living
will.

VIII.29 ✍ PAIN AND FEAR ARE TWO OF THE MOST
basic elements of our physiological and psychological equipment,
for they preserve us from danger. Yet man has, to some extent
in balance with these sensations, the knowledge that he will someday die and that life will go on without him. The life-prolonging
instincts and the sense of death's inevitability can coexist without
friction in almost all individuals except those who, for one reason
or another, know that they must die prematurely and quite soon.
Here the sense of inevitable death and the equally inalienable instinct to continue living confront each other absurdly. The can-
cer victim regularly feels intense pain, but his mind and body are
unable to answer the signal with appropriate action. The man condemned to death feels fear but cannot flee. The exercise of will is
simultaneously evoked and thwarted; the future is simultaneously
entreated and strangled. The avoidance of this inhuman short-
circuiting of will should be ample enough justification for speedy
punishments. It should also arbitrate against the routine medical
prolongation of life in hopeless cases at modern hospitals.

VIII.30 ✍ THE STOICS COUNSEL US TO
think often of death; and it is well worth remembering why.
Death is our forward profile in time, and its division from life is
as intimate and important as the division between our warm skin
and the outer air. To think of death properly is to experience, in
a new dimension, the limits which define us as individuals; it is
also to feel, again and again, the fragile ecstasy of being alive. It

seems, however, that all but the best of us are destined to be forgetful of death; that we must learn about it again and again, like something dreadful and new, with the passing of loved ones. While on a long trip two years ago, I visited, almost as an afterthought, an old friend, a remarkable woman who had worked brilliantly through her eighties and snatched her last productive years from the teeth of a fatal illness. She was sitting by the window in her dining room, in the very white morning light of northern California in May. She had the grace to thank me for coming; and I thought guiltily that, intent on my own inconsequential business, I had almost forgotten to come at all. She was so thin and pale, her skin so delicate and transparent, that the morning light seemed to penetrate quite through her, at once illuminating her from within and promising the near future when the chair by the window would be empty. Perhaps the easiest way to remind ourselves of death is something like this: to look at a person in a room and at the same moment to imagine the room empty.

IX ⚵ ACHIEVEMENT

IX.1 ⚵   EACH OF US OCCUPIES TWO TEMPORAL modalities of being: one which exists in the present and one which stretches through time to our lives' limits. While the former constantly demands our attention, it is upon the latter that every precept of behavior and hope of happiness is based. Our broader selves are our better selves, and our present attitude toward them is optimally one of attentiveness and humility. Conspicuously admirable people seem to inhabit these broader selves and strike us as living in mansions of time; the rest of us, who give up projects in a day's despair, renounce friendships in anger, follow fads and read magazines as oracles, are pent up in temporal hovels. Characteristically anxious or distracted, we inhabit tiny fractions of our full being; and like small patrols, isolated from the main army and ambushed, we respond weakly and are overcome by the shocks of experience. Self-confidence, on the other hand, often consists merely of the ability to connect our fragmentary present with our wholeness in time, the past and future which give it meaning and importance.

IX.2 ⚵   ACHIEVEMENTS LIKE THE WRITING OF books, the painting of pictures, and indeed all long and cumulative individual efforts, are greater than the individuals who produce them, if we view these individuals at any single point in time. For no one can in a single moment recall the multitude of shapes his mind took during the course of the work, or revive the various intensities of passion and calm which injected themselves into its production, or glow with the incremental power built up by weeks or months of care. The work resembles not the partial man, alone within the minutes, but the whole man, incorporate in time.

IX.3 🖎 IDEALLY, A BOLD AND LAVISHLY imaginative individual should begin a project; a methodical and tireless individual, who stands in awe of his partner's brilliance but is affectionately critical of his excesses and lapses, should be in charge of the middle; and a third individual, patient, elegant and scrupulous, deeply impressed by his colleagues' joint achievement but aware that it will fail without his serene overview and inspired refinements, should complete the work. Even more ideally, these three should be one and the same person.

IX.4 🖎 MALLARMÉ WRITES OF "VIDE PAPIER QUE *la blancheur défend*" (blank paper whose whiteness is forbidding); but generally writers love a blank page, a new pad, a ream of bond. For the freshness and openness of these things is an invitation to freedom and to the magic which makes something of nothing. By extension, something similar can be said about the beginnings of large projects in general. During these times our minds are less constrained and more receptive to discovery; our wills are faced less with binary alternatives than with manifold opportunities. As we progress, we will know our subject better, but we will also have set canons which we are reluctant to transgress. Thus at the beginnings of things it is well to treat ourselves to a luxury of blankness, to go into each day's work without the deadening burdens of continuity, consistency and fixed purpose. Don't look back; you will have time enough for that during later stages. At this point the essential things are amplitude, variety, boldness, imagination. Contradictions are not only allowable but essential; for without them you will almost always fail to transcend your initial understanding.

IX.5 ⚘ SKILLED GENERALS NEVER DRIVE THEIR enemies to desperate action; they advance vigorously but always give their antagonists an opportunity for retreat, surrender or negotiation. This mixture of affirmation and forbearance can also be applied to our attitude toward ourselves. In our projects we should always maintain a sense of the unfinished, a feeling that things are not final and that present action can almost always be improved or surpassed by future action. Characteristically, it is the illusion of finality, the illegitimate impulse to perfection, that renders us feeble and hesitant.

IX.6 ⚘ IF THERE IS ANY POINT IN THE COURSE OF a project when stopping and resting is particularly advisable, it is just before we put the thing into final form. In so doing, we defuse potentially destructive haste and allow for the development of a new perspective.

IX.7 ⚘ THE TEDIOUS EXERCISE NECESSARY FOR initiation into any art — the interminable repetition of functions so simple that they seem almost insignificant — is valuable for two obvious reasons: learning simple things makes us capable of learning more difficult things; and the regimen of exercise, once accepted, becomes the structure of the artist's working life. It is also valuable for one less obvious reason: simple things done well are done as well as complex things; and the experience of doing anything well — from the minor scale to the *Hammerklavier Sonata* — is an irreplaceable event of the spirit.

IX.8 ⚘ EXPERTS AT TIME MANAGEMENT WILL give would-be achievers the following hints:

· Fulfill painful obligations as soon as possible.
· Schedule errands and minor chores together rather than separately.

- Do difficult things before easy things.
- Avoid petty disagreements, and do not become upset when others foment them.
- Make minor decisions quickly, and put them out of your mind.
- In general, do not concern yourself with trivia.
- Refuse, politely but decisively, to accept involvements that would distract you from the purposes you value.
- Seek advice from experts, but otherwise avoid projects whose success depends on the charity or competence of others.
- Work much and regularly, but rest and exercise as much and as regularly as you work.
- Ensure that every important activity receives a large and uninterrupted period of time.
- Sell, give away, or otherwise dispose of your television set.
- Keep a personal file.
- Keep a record of your progress by days, weeks and months.

Sensible advice, you will say, but mere tactics, useless without commitment. In a sense you are right. No transition is consistently more difficult to achieve, painful to repeat or easy to forget than the simple step from inaction into action. But in a deeper sense you are wrong. You will not enjoy what you are doing, or indeed truly know what it is, until you have done it well. Commitment is a by-product of involvement. You must take your first steps in the dark.

IX.9 ✍ PATIENCE IS THE WISDOM OF TIME, THE only channel through which time's expansiveness and quiet power can become properties of human will. The patient worker controls the most extensive dimension of mind and can achieve a kind of greatness even if the mind's other dimensions are narrow (as with native weavers of rugs). The spider, who works minutely and slowly, weaves a giant image of herself and becomes a mighty huntress in time.

IX.10 ✍ PATIENCE IS ALSO THE MORAL VIRTUE which most nearly approaches pure pleasure. Action in concentration, without haste or delay, is action in the fullest possible harmony with time; we step with the most natural human pace and rhythm. We sail with the wind, and though things may move around us, we feel a kind of stillness. Time's longer periods take on a kind of quiet excitement, a shiver in the sunlight; its shorter periods, the minutes of work or thought, are tangible, almost edible. And such times are never crushed in memory. They keep their shape and wholeness and become riches of the past.

IX.11 ✍ DO NOT BE TOO QUICK TO DISTINGUISH patience from eagerness. Unquenchable eagerness, compressed and purified by will, is the only fuel hot enough to drive an individual through the endless ways of patient action. The patient individual has, more than any other, retained or recovered the noble eagerness of the child.

IX.12 ✍ THE DIFFERENCE BETWEEN COMPETENCE and incompetence is no greater than the difference between mere competence and achievement. Real achievement, which augments the sum of human worth and knowledge, is seldom born of a conventional understanding; it is always a shock to the competent who, usually middle-aged, defensive and unprepared for new exertions, depend upon the *status quo* and have come to accept it as representing the limits of the known universe. Achievement often strikes such people with an aversion that is almost chemical, producing in them a giddy fear of chaos. Their response is generally one of sharp challenge, ringing with probity and harboring the threat of ostracism. Thus almost every achiever is, at least temporarily, a kind of minor tragic hero, punished for his contribution; he must with good cheer endure the interval between impact and absorption.

IX.13 ✍ ARGUE FOR WHAT YOU BELIEVE TO BE true, but never expect to win an important point with words alone.

Valuable theses are not proven by unassisted reason but rather by concoctions of reason and time — words forcefully and quotably phrased, calmly delivered in speech and writing, patiently repeated at intervals. Indeed, you know the truth only when you know the truth about truth, which is that it is often startlingly unfamiliar to its audience, that it is not self-evident but becomes clear only through repeated contact, and that its bearers must be not only perceptive but also persistent. People are not convinced by the truth so much as inhabited and colonized by it; they will not come back to you and say that you were right so much as they will, after lengthy periods of incubation, repeat your ideas to you as though they had thought them up themselves. By the same token, distrust an individual who rushes his proof or your response to it. This is no teacher but rather a salesman, who is right, if at all, only partially and by chance.

IX.14 ✍ TIME IS ENDLESS WHEN IT IS ADEQUATE. For in one sense time exists only in relation to what is willed and done; and the act of completing something is like closing a circle in nature.

IX.15 ✍ IT IS COMMON FOR INDIVIDUALS, AFTER some great success, to take a "well-earned" rest; while other individuals, having experienced major setbacks, feel impelled to renew activity and involvement as soon as they possibly can. Both these desires are psychologically warranted and carry strong social approval; but there is a good case to be made for precisely the opposite course of action. During and just after great victories we are most likely to possess the imagination for new ideas, the self-respect to nurture them and the strength to give them substance. Like loaded trucks which have at last reached turnpike speed, or runners who have gotten second wind, we have achieved a sovereign pace; our psychological mass (to borrow one of Einstein's laws) is increased proportionally to our motion. These are the best times to begin new things. Conversely, it is after failed efforts that we should rest. A failure is like a jolting full stop, a sudden and useless exhaustion of energy. It calls for a recouping of power and a review of direction, rather than for sudden choices and bold risks. Intense activity after failure saps the spirit and, because it is a classic form of haste, opens up a gallery of potential errors. Repose after failure shows conquest of embarrassment and confidence in the future; it is a mark of dignity and basic health. Moreover, the analysis of failure is an indispensable activity which demands leisure and time.

IX.16 ✍ SUCCESSFUL PEOPLE GENERALLY HAVE more errors to their credit, and often bigger ones, than unsuccessful people. They view these in the same way that scientists view failed experiments: not as moral setbacks but as the necssary concomitants of discovery. While plodders see failure as a demon, achievers see it more as a void, oppressive perhaps but not intimidating, and capable of redemption by the first success that comes along. They know, however, that success, no matter how much praised or how well rewarded, will open up new challenges, new risks of failure.

IX.17 ✍ SOCIETY MAINTAINS NO VERBAL apparatus so extensive or complex as that which excuses the lack of achievement.

IX.18 ✍ HEARING THE PORTENTOUS MOTTO "Learn from your own errors," our natural response is "Learn what?" The commonest errors are mere lapses, mistakes born of distraction or of the momentary relaxation of mind against the hard surface of experience. Such errors are mere facts of nature, as statistically unavoidable as they are specifically unpredictable. But we *can* learn something about the causes of error and the moments which favor it. The former are fairly well known: fatigue, haste, anxiety, overconfidence, passion, imperfect preparation. But the latter are less often discussed. We tend to err at the beginnings of actions, when we are unused to the demands and limita-tions of a new context. We tend to err near the end of actions, by hurrying to finish or relaxing too soon. We err after periods of stress, whether or not this stress has produced successful results. And most dangerously we err after our own errors, either by try-ing to correct them too quickly, or by swerving rashly in the op-posite direction, or by retreating into a callow and doomed cor-rectness, or by espousing our errors and defending them from all comers.

IX.19 ✍ THE YEARS FORGET OUR ERRORS AND forgive our sins, but they punish our inaction with living death.

IX.20 ✍ ON SOME DAYS, AND PARTICULARLY during the daylight hours, I am possessed by a curious feeling I call "towardness," a feeling of something quite wonderful just about to happen — some letter, telegram or phone call laden with miraculous tidings — as though a warm future had suddenly taken on mass and volume and was pressing amorously against my men-tal space. And though I have had this feeling scores of times, I can say without hesitation that not a single exceptionally good thing ever happened to me on any of those days. In fact, I got no benefit at all from these moods until I realized that the signals were coming not from the future but from the present, not from the outside but from the inside; that they were signals not to wait and receive but to labor and achieve.

IX.21 ✍ IT IS NOT ONLY THE BACKSWING AND the impact that determine good strokes in tennis, but also the fol-lowing through. In other words, the course, speed and trajectory of the ball are partly governed by what the racket does *after* im-pact. Analogously, the boxer learns to aim his blows, not at the point of contact, but somewhat beyond it; and the karate master practices similar methods. The same rule holds in many other forms of experience. People of understanding do not aim at actions so much as through them; others, who desist from effort at the supposed moment of completion, often complete nothing at all and almost never learn from their success or failure. Recovering from a medically treated disease, Mr. A heaves a sigh of relief and sets about forgetting the symptoms and treatment as soon as possible; Mr. B, similarly afflicted and cured, reviews his symptoms and prescriptions and tries to commit all to memory. Authors A and B receive long and detailed letters of rejection from the same publisher. A reads his letter cursorily and prepares to submit his manuscript elsewhere; B reads his letter carefully, notes the important points and writes a brief response. On the last day of a group project, Chairman A dismisses his committee, files his records and turns to the next piece of business; Chairman B reviews his file and calls a brief meeting to thank his colleagues and analyze the treatment of the project.

For the A's of the world, each experience is distinct from the flow of life, and they view each in terms of "goals" or "episodes" which must be "attained" or "finished." B's, on the other hand, understand that particular experiences are all part of a broader context of analogies, recurrences and contrasts; that present success or failure, pleasure or pain, can be used to plot lines on the map of the future. A particular illness may strike the same person twice. Editors who reject manuscripts sometimes do so with very good reason; they will often accept revised work or a new manuscript from a previously-rejected author. The review of joint projects is an education in analysis, interaction and leadership. This may sound like mere common sense, but in fact it represents a comprehensive departure from the popular view of time. Like children at an amusement park, carted past bright-colored flat cardboard props, the A's see experience two-dimensionally; the future and present are clearly lit for them, but the past is blackness. The B's see and feel the wholeness of things in time.

IX.22   THERE IS A SURPRISINGLY GREAT difference, in terms of psychological dynamics, between accepting the fact that we must perform a certain action in the future and deciding exactly when we are going to do it. In the former case, we merely acknowledge a need, leaving ourselves free to temporize with it as our impulses dictate; in the latter, we seem to be making the action a part of ourselves, assuming it within our physical identity. In this sense, planning is a true extension of identity in time, control not only of external events but of inner resources.

IX.23 ⚑ MUCH OF OUR DAILY QUOTA OF ENERGY is spent in making adjustments, corrections and repairs — retrieving and reviewing lost trains of thought, reorganizing after interruptions, resisting the intrusion of irrelevancies, suppressing emotional revolts, negotiating with fantasies. Like climbers on a mountain of soft sand, we slide back seven steps for every eight we gain, struggling over familiar ground and arriving almost exhausted at our point of departure. The mind with the modest talent of moving consecutively from point to point is so rare that it is considered brilliant. Only such minds can begin to enjoy the capacious and varied fullness of time; for the rest of us, time is scattered by distraction, blotted out by repetition.

IX.24 ⚑ ALL IMPORTANT ACTIONS ARE open-ended to the future. Once accomplished, they continue to vibrate in time, not only in the sense that they generate other actions, but in the sense that they become available through memory to a will which can learn from them, reject them or reinterpret and remake them. A young physicist discovers a new particle and wins the Nobel Prize; twenty years later, this past achievement can either give him magnificent confidence or convince him that he is no longer the man he once was. A man can renounce his youthful follies as the work of another identity or accept them as early signs of the vigor which, more directedly, has fueled his subsequent achievements. We revise our earlier lives the way authors revise their works, patching, expurgating, suppressing, retitling the past. And in this sense the past is never over, affecting us even (and particularly) when we deny it.

IX.25 ✒ OF ALL AMBITIONS, PERHAPS THE LEAST
practicable is that of regaining something that has been lost — a
love, a trust, or any other desirable state of affairs. Even things
retained change from day to day; lost things change far more strik-
ingly, not only in the minds of others but in our own. Since half of
what we lost was our own spirit of possessing and participating in
it, the thing is not merely lost, but in effect ceases to be. The means
by which things were originally gained are immensely subtle; and
even if we could consciously duplicate them, change would probably have rendered them invalid. That which we won and held by
luck, confidence and simple good humor is far less available to the
strained pleading of the dispossessed; just as the gift has become a
different one, we now seem different to the giver. Finally, and even
more basically, do we really want this thing back, or are we only
trying to prove that we deserved it? Do we want back what we had
or what we think we had? Accepting loss is an art which is among
the few really attractive secrets of maturity.

If, after all this, you are still determined to recoup some loss,
there is only one course to follow: treat what you lost as something
entirely new and potentially better than what you had before. You
will be more likely to get what you are after, and you will also be
correct.

IX.26 ✒ THERE ARE PEOPLE WHOSE PRIVATE
work occupies them so thoroughly that they have little time to
spare for love or fellowship, and people who are so continuously
loving and fellowly that they cannot get on with their work. Without going into the psychology of such types, it is possible to say
that in both cases their lot would be improved if they learned to
give each activity *undivided* time. A few hours of good work a
day can satisfy our professional obligations and exhaust our best
energies. A few hours of concentrated philanthropy and love can
ease our hearts' burdens and satisfy (if not indeed inundate) the
people around us.

IX.27 ✒ DURING THE 1960s, AN AMERICAN
university administrator, profoundly irritated by the radical out-

bursts of a member of his faculty, took the novel step of putting the man in a post of some authority in the very area of affairs he had been complaining about. Suddenly transposed from a position of relative license to one of communal responsibility, the professor underwent a remarkable change of heart and speedily turned his attention to conservative polemics. While it is hard not to admire the senior administrator's ironic prescience, we must also see this incident as an example of the generally muffling and subduing effect which promotion and authority can have on active people. Such honors, while usually intended to reward achievers, are actually punishments, in that the honors deprive them of the time and energy for continued achievement in their fields. Moreover, the assumption that a brilliant scholar or scientist will also be an effective administrator is manifestly fallacious. Political achievement, as we have just seen, often calls less for rational preeminence than for a rare sensibility which is at once dogged and poetic. If they lack such virtue, achievers in special fields would do well to stay out of administration; avoiding also, insofar as possible, the committees and commissions, workshops and lecture tours, which success will inevitably dish up. They should accept for their work only such rewards as will enable them to continue its development.

IX.28 ✍ ON MEETING PEOPLE RENOWNED FOR achievement, we are often surprised (and perhaps comforted) by how human and fallible they seem. The great scholar errs about a date; the moralist has a chronic twitch; the chief executive indulges in an inept witticism or commits a grammatical blunder. Conversely, we are often stunned by the brilliance, or humbled by the correctness, of individuals who, we later discover, have achieved little or nothing. Behind this paradox lies one of the mysteries of achievement: that it seems to be won less by intensity than by integrity, less by aggressive assaults than by concentration indefinitely and heroically prolonged in time. Individuals who seek gain of a relatively momentary nature regularly short-circuit their own concentration and defeat themselves in the continuum; indeed, some of their verbal sharpness may be fueled by the petulant awareness of their failure in the larger sphere. Preeminent individuals, whatever their attitude toward instants and moments, *exist* more in the larger chambers and outdoor stretches of time than in its fractions and compartments. They are the through-traffic of life, while we others are condemned to creep along the business routes.

IX.29 ✍︎   THE MIND WHICH CAN TOTALLY AND inanely forget its work and obligations is often also the mind which can, at the proper time, give them the fullest attention. People of this bent know not only the value of concentration but also the secret resource of fallowness. They protect their fragile hours of productivity with down pillows of oblivion.

IX.30 ✍︎   ANYONE WHO APPLIES HIMSELF regularly, lengthily and energetically to a single project is certain, no matter what else happens, to encounter days of profound delight or unprecedented inspiration.

X ✒ TIME
AND ART

X.1 ✒ GOOD ARTISTS, EVEN THOSE WHO work very quickly, turn to every detail, every passage, as though it could if necessary be given an infinite amount of time. This readiness to delay paradoxically adds to their effective speed; for the awareness that they will never let pressures of time cheapen their efforts gives them confidence and hence pace. This fact stands behind the many adages which relate achievement to patience. Patience is no more than generosity with time; and the artist who is generous with time will be rewarded in turn. This is truest under the most extreme conditions, when the artist faces heavy difficulties and the project seems almost dead in the water. Here whole days seem barren; and despair beckons continually, in the form of total surrender, seductive distractions or voguish and facile charades of meaning. The patience shown at this point — the experiments, false starts, trashings and reconsiderations which may take weeks — is probably the best-spent effort in the whole achievement; for aside from its material results, it is an irreplaceable affirmation of commitment.

X.2 ✒ AVOID WORRYING ABOUT WHETHER WHAT you write will be worth reading. Instead ask whether it is worth writing; and, if so, how it may best be written. Avoid worrying about whether what you write will be original. When originality occurs at all (which is rare), it occurs as a by-product of conviction.

x.3 🖎 ANTHONY TROLLOPE WROTE EVERY morning before going off to work for the postal service. His attitude toward his art was placid and workmanlike: he set himself weekly quotas in pages, and if he happened to complete a book during the course of a morning's work, he would simply begin another. His contemporary Gustave Flaubert would sit each day for hours, fuming, fretting and scribbling words and phrases, until the proper rhythms and tonalities broke surface in his mind. Then, for a relatively short period, he would write fluently and intensely. Trollope and Flaubert had little in common except that, like all successful artists, they viewed time heroically and made themselves lavish gifts of it. They understood that no artistic necessity — not technique, elegance, genius itself — is more basic or inalienable than regular and expansive time. One need not be great or famous to experience its positive force. To sit down at your desk in the morning and know that you are taking up the work of a thousand mornings, to write knowing that tomorrow's work can redeem any imperfection in today's — these realizations produce cheer and confidence in and of themselves. Similarly, when we allow ourselves not just one or two hours, but several for productive activity, we show patience and mercy to our own minds, and they bring forth good things even on bad days. And building thus in time prepares the ground for an uncommon pleasure — that sense of unique commitment, integral and resolute, which seems the property of good artists. For such a deep and general commitment is no more than the sum of countless humbler commitments, regularly made and sincerely kept.

x.4 🖎 LAUGHABLE ERROR AND PROFOUND discovery are born of the same freedom.

x.5 🖎 TO YOUNG WRITERS, THE BULK AND variety of already-published work often produces the impression that everything has been done — that there is nothing left for them to do except imitate or qualify the past. This sentiment, moreover, is fostered by critics, who necessarily spend most of their time evaluating ideas which are already a few years old and who are thus professionally fixated on the immediate past; and by those editors who discard literary proposals because, "That is not what people are reading these days." Writers who suffer from this intimidating illusion would do well to remember the following:

The published writing of a given era, no matter how comprehensive it may seem to be, is generally based on shared assumptions, and therefore suffers from common weaknesses.

The surface of the human condition, vexed and driven by change, incessantly demands new patterns of art.

While the reading public and those who purvey to it may seem to dominate the present, the future is the domain of sincere and persistent individuals.

x.6   A SELDOM-MENTIONED VIRTUE OF paperback books is that their flimsy constitution generally prevents them from outlasting their authors' reputations.

x.7   THE PROPER GOAL OF ALL TECHNICAL refinement in art is a style which is authentic. The artistic portrayal of phenomena, no matter how energetic, polished or detailed it may be, is empty of meaning unless it reveals, as in a kind of inner painting, the awareness perceiving these phenomena, the receptive spirit at its profoundest level of activity. And this revelation of identity is not truly authentic unless it is somehow familiar to its audience and shared by them. For the good artist has two identities — individuality and humanity — and cannot produce well unless he reveals both. Indeed, authenticity is no more than a rare and precious form of communality, brought into focus by individual experience. One of the reasons why there is so little good art is that few artists are capable of expressing both of these identities. Those who think in the communal style can conceive of no other; while those who despise it fail to see that it holds, in its very creases and foibles, the inalienable channels of poetry.

X.8 🖎 THE STATUS QUO IS THE STRAIGHT MAN of history; the changing patterns of wit which dapple the ages always play off against it. More specifically, wit is the dynamic friction between two forms of seriousness: a lower seriousness which is the wisdom of the times, affected, self-righteous and devoutly studious of trifles, and a higher seriousness, which claims reference to unchanging humanity. Ages like our own, which for all their published chatter have about as much true wit as a duck has teeth, are barren of fun because they are impoverished of seriousness.

X.9 🖎 THE MODERN CRITIQUE OF ART ON THE basis of natural or social science — whether psychology, sociology, sociobiology, economics or some other — is as effective as a critique of athletics by a nutritionist. Basic points of connection are undeniable; but there are huge gaps between these and a total understanding, and lost among these is the experience of art, whether by artist or audience, as an act of freedom.

X.10 🖎 HAMLET, WHO SAID THAT ART HOLDS "the mirror up to nature," was describing art's apparent function rather than its inner design. It is science which takes on, as faithfully as possible, the image of nature. In art, on the other hand, images of nature are shaped to conform to the structure of mind. The work of art, like some delicate wax mold, is contrived to fit a channel of perception, a matrix of psychological experience; like a master key, it can unlock, in different individuals, similar responses. Thus great art, no matter what its external shape or detail, has at heart, in a coded pattern of appeal, the inverse structure of mental principle, the shape and rhythm of pure mind. This form can be particular or general. Smaller works of art — a Schubert song, an ode by Horace, a red-figure vase — unlock intense but limited responses. Massive works — *Paradise Lost*, the *Messiah*, the *Last Judgement* — invade and populate whole provinces of mind. It is possible to conceive of an art form so expansive and multileveled that it comprises, at least in terms of its abstract dynamics, the total portraiture of thought. Such a concept figures, though very vaguely, in the game called the *Glasperlenspiel* of Hermann Hesse's novel of the same name. It occurs in Plato's concept of dialectic and in the sum total of his works. And it is suggested in the combinations of symmetry and contrast, repose and wonderment, in a great formal garden.

X.11 ✍ FEW OCCURRENCES ARE SO PROFOUNDLY shocking as the intrusion of one dimension of time upon another. When someone expected late returns early, when a new piece of equipment fails, when the present takes on momentary but unmistakable attributes of the past (*déjà vu*), when we discover some long-hidden relic of childhood, we stagger and are briefly lost in time. Momentarily we exist at two times at once; and the rock of present time, that firm context which defines our normal perceptions, dissolves beneath our feet. Are these experiences aberrations, illusions of a transtemporality which does not in fact exist? On the contrary, I think instead that they are *revelations*, rare visions of the full volume and unified scope of time. For an instant we step outside of ourselves and are blinkingly aware of the wildly grander reality which surrounds us. It is as though we were able to stand in two places at once — to see the placid unity of space, which includes all viewpoints yet denies the validity of any single one. Thus to leave our present self is to sense, if only imperfectly, a far more extensive self, a fuller aspect of identity which is no less urgent for being so often ignored. And this enlightening transtemporality, here triggered by chance, can also be achieved through contemplation or, in some cases, by art.

X.12 ✍ GREAT DRAMATIC ART IS TRANSTEMPORAL in two specific senses: fictive and psychological.

FICTIVE TRANSTEMPORALITY

Every dramatist may exploit four temporal modalities, and these may be complementary or contradictory:

1. Physical time — the actual length of the performance
2. Hypothetical time — the supposed duration of the action
3. Dynamic time — the pace of the action
4. Allusive time — the use of time as an image or subject of discussion on stage

In *Romeo and Juliet,* physical time is the "two hours' traffic" of the performance as referred to by the Prologue. Hypothetical time is the few days between the first Montague-Capulet skirmish on a Verona street and the final scene in the Capulet tomb. Dynamic time springs from the distinction between the relatively slow-paced early scenes and the speeding up of the action after Tybalt's death in act 3. Allusive time exists in Romeo's characteristic haste, his gloomy utterances about the future, the Nurse's description of a scene from Juliet's childhood, the Prologue's mere mention, on stage, of "two hours' traffic." Transtemporality can be achieved by setting off one of these modalities against another (so that, for example, we "see" the adolescent Juliet and her three-year-old prior self at the same time) or by telescoping time so that consequence follows immediately upon action and an essential tragic structure is revealed. This latter device involves the obliteration of normal present-oriented time and the revelation of a broader scheme whose unique signposts and boundaries are the defining attributes of individual character and will. This form of transtemporality occurs brilliantly in Samuel Beckett's *Krapp's Last Tape.* Here the fiction concerns a man who, having tape-recorded his thoughts on many preceding birthdays, reviews them tragically at the end of his life.

X.13 ✎ PSYCHOLOGICAL TRANSTEMPORALITY, THE second form of dramatic transtemporality, involves the simultaneous evocation of psychological modalities which in normal life tend to occur only one at a time. In *Macbeth,* for example, we can share the corrupted but intensely human awareness of the hero, the guilt-stricken despair of his wife, and the amply justified moral outrage of his enemies. In *Othello,* we have vivid contact with the injured innocence of Desdemona, the nihilistic loathing of Iago and the remarkable disorder of love and rage, manliness and insecurity in Othello himself. The fact that these emotions may be completely contrary to each other means nothing to us at all; we accept them because they are profoundly familiar to us, hallmarks of archetypal humanity. In normal life, as I have argued earlier, our experience of each modality is temporally far separate from our experience of any other; and when we indulge any one of our propensities, we tend to forget all the others. We are brave and cowardly, generous and destructive, lovers and haters by fits and starts. Isolated in single modalities, we forget our inconsistency and the kaleidoscopic versatility of our natures; to this extent we can become creatures of circumstance if not unconciousness hypocrites. Shakespeare's genius — indeed his majesty as a moral artist — lies in his ability to overcome this temporal blindness, to set before us the brilliant and dreadful multiplicity of our spirit.

X.14 ✍ GREAT ART IS AS ELEGANT IN ITS structure as in its detail; but structure is so wedded to detail as to be hard to discover. Detail in art must seem natural, inevitable; the larger design which makes this possible must be at once muscular and unobtrusive, artful and artless. In Italian Renaissance painting, structure — the basic pattern of light against dark — is concealed beneath brilliant color, dramatic human characterization and the illusion of perspective. To perceive the structure of such art, the observer should, like some lunatic or Philistine, stand back and squint, until the more obvious phenomena are obscured and the basic design is available. Without such an understanding, a full appreciation of the work is impossible. Similar dynamics apply to the study of music, drama and literature; though here, where the work of art is not apparent to a glance but rather stretches through time, we must squint cerebrally rather than optically. In literature we must become sensible to the massive elements which most readers take for granted — location, number of characters, duration, transition. We must resist the power of the fiction to listen for the subtle and relentless return of phrases, tonalities, attributes and ideas which is the author's only way of establishing sculptural unity in a temporal work. We must step backward in time, reviewing the work in our minds, days, weeks or months after reading, until details have sifted into oblivion and only a general impression remains. In so doing, we will with practice learn to see the invisible, to hear beneath the surface phrases that quiet pulse of universal meaning which is the secret of great art.

X.15 ✍ THOSE PILGRIMS WHO, AS IS CUSTOMARY, place all their hopes in arriving at some wished-for chapel or shrine, are unaware of the true purpose of their pilgrimage; for the fulfillment of that purpose resides equally in the exhausting approach, the chosen encounter and the silent journey home. Similar are the readers who, enthralled by some work of literature, race through it with all thoughts concentrated on the story's end. They miss the real end, the final cause and full pleasure of the work, which as Conrad tells us is in every line. Intent on the temporal or sequential structure of the story or poem, they miss its spatial structure, which exists all at once and as though outside of time; they enjoy the product of art but are blind to the art itself.

X.16 ✍ THE GREATEST PHILOSOPHERS TOOK pains not to be quotable; they expressed their most serious ideas not through direct statement but rather through implication, allusion, repetition, contrast, symbol, irony and context; they floated their proofs in time. To them the concise explanation was anathema, the accommodating professor as undesirable as a jeering mob.

X.17 ✍ WRITTEN TRUTH IS FOUR-DIMENSIONAL. If we consult it at the wrong time, or read it at the wrong pace, it is as empty and shapeless as a dress on a hook.

X.18 ✍ PERHAPS MORE THAN ANY OTHER engineer of his time, Rudolf Diesel was successful in developing mechanical processes which converted matter into usable energy with minimum loss. Posing the same problem in terms of less mechanical projects, we find that it is usually the individual, working toward some specific and exclusive goal, who comes closest to attaining Diesel's ideal, while group enterprises tend to fall far short. The group — a committee, for example — wastes energy deciding its goals and methods, synchronizing its efforts, keeping itself informed and being polite to itself. Like an engine with ill-fitting pistons, it cannot convert authority into power without friction. The individual — an artist, for example — is like a demigod, not omnipotent, but magnificently free. Given time and a healthy will, he is limited by nothing but the dynamics of his medium. He can convert decision into action instantaneously; he can tyrannize and humiliate himself without apology, in the name of a higher justice. His dignity, if it matters to him at all, lies in this very liberty, directness and application. And while the committee is confused and distressed after failure, the artist is not. Sure of his values and intentions, he is as justified by what he attempts as by what he achieves. This achievement, moreover, is at its best the ultimate capture of energy: for at its best, a work of art is like a perpetual motion machine, or a beam of light caught forever in a palace of mirrors.

X.19   THE SIMPLEST FORM OF CREATIVE expression available to most of us is the letter. Letters may take an hour or less to write; but a number of them (for example, those of Plato, Cicero and Pliny the Younger) have endured for millennia. Whether we write for permanence or merely for communication, the act of producing a letter, even one which is never mailed, necessitates a form of creative concentration which can improve our lives. Copies of our own letters are useful for our records and memories. If their recipients think them worth saving, they can have value and effect far beyond that of the spoken word. In friendship, the letter is not only a message but a gift, a physical symbol of esteem and affection. In business or politics, the letter can not only express the concerns of the moment but remain as a document of such concerns, available for prolonged scrutiny by more than one reader. Moreover, while speakers and listeners in a debate are vulnerable to emotion and subject to fallacy, the well-written letter remains calm and crisp and is subject to nothing except superior reason. It can convince the open-minded, goad the weak-hearted, give our opponents an exact index of the level and intensity of our commitment, and be quoted by those who agree with us. But perhaps most importantly, our letters are the proof and body of our concern for life in its detail and our convinction that this concern should be shared with others. The hero of Cocteau's *Les Enfants Terribles* writes the most important letter of his life and then absentmindedly addresses it to himself. In so doing he symbolizes the reflective and self-engendering function of the letter and of art in general.

X.20   FORM IS AT ITS BEST A MEANINGFUL assortment of oppositions — light and dark, fast and slow, serious and comic, orderly and chaotic. Without this dynamic formal interplay, the sublimest vision and the earthiest realization are equally empty of power. The artist who cannot establish a context of expectation can never surprise. The artist who cannot compel seriousness can never command irony. The artist immune to violence is incapable of peace. The artist who cannot repeat cannot vary.

X.21   TEN YEARS FROM NOW I MAY ENJOY these writings, or find them worthless. But there is no guarantee that my future critical faculties will be at all applicable to my present work, or that I will have any more insight into subject or style than I do at present. We must at once labor for the future and disregard its potential consequences.

X.22   IF YOU ARE PLANNING TO WRITE FICTION, do not sit around too long trying to think up a good story. If you work hard, the story will come to life as you are writing it. Remember also that all decent fiction has the same inner story: the story of discovery.

x.23 🖋 SPEAK OF LITERARY ART AS TEACHING, delighting, celebrating, communicating, preserving, convincing. But speak of it also as gift-giving, the shy gift-giving of intensely sociable people.

JOURNAL OF THIS BOOK

x.24 🖋 SINCE BEGINNING WORK ON THIS manuscript I have kept a lengthy journal whose chief purpose has been to record the conditions of my work and my thoughts about it as it developed. I am going to include a number of entries from it here, not as a commentary on the manuscript but rather as a part of it. My aim is to show that this, like other works of its kind, is curiously introspective: that what I am writing is also what I am writing about.

OCTOBER 24, 1978 (LA HERRADURA, GRANADA, Spain). The first week of writing at La Herradura. The day: I rise about 8, wash, breakfast with my family til 9:30. Then I go up to the quiet room on the upper floor (this house has two disconnected floors) and write for about three hours. Then we lunch. The afternoons are free. We often nap after lunch; almost always (except that my son Anthony is now ill) we drive down to the village to shop and swim in the sea. At about 5 I jog around these hills for twenty to twenty-five minutes. Then a shower and cocktails at sunset.

After breakfast or lunch I spend about thirty minutes studying Spanish.

I plan to continue this style of life for ten more months.

After dinner I read. I am in the middle of four different books: Gay Wilson Allen's biography of William James, Trollope's *The Warden*, a tedious spy novel and Irving's *Tales of the Alhambra*.

During these sunny days, as I begin work on a book about whose practical value I have not the slightest idea, I am struck again and again by what a fortunate life I have. My days are an unqualified pleasure. There is not a moment of time-killing or enervating routine. Nearly everything, from writing to brushing my teeth, brings a special excitement or comfort. Activities like work, swimming or reading are isolated so that each recurs with a measure of novelty. They are prolonged enough to create, within a single day, a number of separate spheres of experience. This last point is important to me. When I spend my day homogeneously, typing or socializing, doing research or administration, I feel walled into a part of myself, isolated from the totality.

When I say that I am fortunate, I do not mean that all this came as a gift. To bring it about, I borrowed as much money as I normally make in a year. I did not borrow this money in order to write a book. I borrowed it in order to have free time.

X.25 ⚞ JANUARY–MAY, 1979 (CARMEL VALLEY, California). Just as I finished that last sentence, my wife called from downstairs to tell me that our son was so ill as to warrant a trip to the hospital in Granada. Three weeks later we left Spain to see doctors in America. Now he is well again, and we have settled here in the country to spend the rest of our free year. . . . I write with felt-tipped pen in two legal-size Spanish notebooks. I enter writings of uneven length into thirty-five subject headings which never seem to be getting much fuller. . . . Now, after about 500 entries and six months, I am still in the confused beginnings and have successfully cultivated an oblivious attitude toward writing in which one day's work is immediately forgotten, and each day the whole book starts anew. No end in sight to this stage, nor any idea what the finished product will look like. . . . Pale, foggy light in this almost-bare room. I sit on two faded red chairs by a large window — butt on one chair, legs on the other, notebooks held on crossed legs. The room about 12 × 12 feet, facing south; the house typical California tract style of the 1960s: marbled linoleum floors set in square tiles, sheet-rock walls painted (by amateurs) a pleasant sky blue. The window looks out on the ascending row of Monterey pines which the owners of this house, now divorced, planted each Christmas for years. The morning fog is lifting; the weather will almost certainly clear and bring another brilliant spring day. I am ready for work, full of coffee and tinned ham, my indispensable morning cigar waiting on the sill. And after work, the pleasant succession of lunch, sunbath, afternoon with the family, jog in Garland Ranch Park.

X.26 𝄃 JANUARY 3, 1980 (EUGENE, OREGON). Back at work. Confusion continues, with weeks so shattered that they do not even form cohesive history but crumble into rubble like unbaked bricks. I had only about five days of writing in December, then graded papers until the seventeenth. Our plans about where to spend the Christmas holiday changed and rechanged. After the seventeenth we all got ill for a week, and on the twenty-third we gave up all holiday travel plans. On the twenty-eighth I left alone for three days in San Francisco to attend a conference. I arrived back in Eugene on the thirty-first, tired and depressed. Part of my depression touched surface in a dream I had at the end of an almost sleepless night. It was set in this house. An entire guerrilla force had holed up in my little study and from there was engaging a determined government patrol with explosive weapons large and small. From a near-by room I listened to this hell breaking loose and suddenly remembered that this manuscript remained where I had left it on an upper bookshelf in the study. A desperate fear and confusion came over me.

So it stands with my work and the things which keep me from it.

X.27 𝄃 APRIL 16, 1980 (EUGENE, OREGON). The manuscript sample has now been at ——— [publishers] for six weeks — two weeks beyond the amount of time they were supposed to need. I wait; I approach my office mailbox as though it contained a bomb. Here I should be writing original and intelligent remarks about how it feels for an author to be *waiting* for news about his book on *time*. I have no intelligent remarks to make. The project is no longer, as it was a year ago, a free initiative. Even though it is going well presently, it has gotten involved in the less free aspects of my life — the need for money, the dependence on and anxiety about the approval of the outside world, the general hopes and fears. As before, I feel at times that the book is very bad and at times that it is very good; an ambiguity complicated by the fact that, if very bad, it may still be successful; if very good, still rejected. Chiefly for reasons of self-defense, I expect a rejection.

x.28 ✍ MAY 26, 1980 (EUGENE, OREGON).
This year I have been giving classes on Tuesdays and Thursdays
and have established Friday–Saturday–Sunday–Monday as a four-
day writing week. On a writing day I rise between six and eight
(depending on whether or not it is my turn to take care of the
children) and am here in my study by nine, with more than four
hours of uninterrupted free time ahead of me. I sit down in my
easy chair, light a cigar and examine my ragged Spanish notebooks
for likely entries to type up. I smoke and daydream and brood. I
find sections that interest me and then sit worrying about their
quality. I let a number of miscellaneous pains, memories and long-
ings work their way through my system. After about an hour of
this I move over to a corner of the room where an IBM Selectric
typewriter sits on a homemade mahogany-fir typing table. My
cigar comes along, to be puffed on during the moments of imbecile
helplessness that are bound to occur in the course of work. I sit
down to write, and I do so. When I am done, I leave the study and
relax into the sloppy, pleasant routine of daily life. Imbecile helplessness aside, I can hardly think of two people more different from
each other than I when I am writing and I when I am not. It is as
though foggy twilight were temporarily concentrated into a re-
spectable beam of light. Through blind faith and brutal concentration I can regain touch with the serious worker who has written
before and will write again; I can abandon my present feebleness
and connect with my temporally extensive strength.

x.29 ✍ AUGUST 12, 1980 (EUGENE, OREGON).
——— [publisher] has turned us down. The letter doubted that
the book would sell and spoke of problems with format. I was particularly appalled by the comment that a decently written (as he
admitted) book about time would not sell. I think he really meant
that he was not about to risk his money on an unknown author, no
matter what the book. Now I need no longer haunt my office mailbox for letters. Now I must consult my own handbook for ways
of taking reverses.

X.30 ✍ JANUARY 24, 1981. I FINISHED THE typing yesterday and am now in the middle of numbering pages, and everything will go off to a literary agent next week. I look forward now to days of passive excitement and anxiety, and beyond that to the success that will, in a single instant, cork up a whole period of my life, or the failure which will diffuse itself over months of kid-gloved torture, of varying and declining hope. Win or lose, I will have to find some new future to daydream about. Win or lose, I will be spiritually out of work and will hunt after some new project like a day-laborer looking for a new boss.

XI ⚘ ⚘ ⚘ NATURAL AND UNNATURAL TIME ⚘ ⚘ ⚘ ⚘ ⚘ ⚘

XI.I ⚘ OUR BASIC PATTERNS OF COGNITION AND communication — languages, number systems, modes of analysis — may be compared to windows through which we apprehend nature and experience and through which we may, in turn, communicate our findings to others. The clearness and brilliance of these windows, their ability to convey reality faithfully and effectively, depends on two critical factors: (1) the accuracy with which a particular system can describe the characteristics of phenomena, and (2) the system's aptness to the dynamics of the mind. These two factors often overlap, but they are by no means synonymous. The binary number system, for example — in which any number can be expressed by a combination or multiple of only two symbols — is a highly accurate method of counting which is nonetheless poorly adapted to conscious thought and language. The Ptolemaic cosmology, on the other hand, was an harmonious and communicable system which happened to be an almost total perversion of reality. In general, our methods of keeping, calculating and communicating time fall into the first category. They are accurate but unwieldy — often to the point of uselessness and frustration.

XI.2 ⚘ OUR UNITS OF TEMPORAL MEASUREMENT, from seconds on up to months, are so complicated, asymmetrical and disjunctive as to make coherent mental reckoning in time all but impossible. Indeed, had some tyrannical god contrived to enslave our minds to time, to make it all but impossible for us to escape subjection to sodden routines and unpleasant surprises, he could hardly have done better than handing down our present system. It is like a set of trapezoidal building blocks, with no vertical or horizontal surfaces, like a language in which the simplest thought demands ornate constructions, useless particles and lengthy circumlocutions. Unlike the more successful patterns of language and science, which enable us to face experience boldly or at least levelheadedly, our system of temporal calculation silently and persistently encourages our terror of time.

XI.3 ⚹ AN EXECUTIVE, SCHEDULING A BUSINESS trip, wishes to know in March what day of the week May 15 will fall on. A house party is planned, one month in advance, for the second weekend in August; and we do not know the date. A professor is setting up his lectures in advance, or trying to discover what he said in the second lecture of the last term. All these relatively simple calculations are, because of our present system of reckoning, usually impossible without a calendar. But these problems are only tell-tales of a general discomfort we feel toward the passage of seconds, minutes, hours, days, weeks and months. Though we have been taught to think in the decimal system, our subdiurnal measurements are parceled up into ungainly bunches of 60's and 12's. The week is an arbitrary construct based on the most intractable number in the decimal system and having no relationship whatsoever to astronomical time or to the encompassing sequence of months. The months are almost equally arbitrary and, what is worse, of varying lengths. The effect of these manifold irregularities is that we not only have great difficulty in reckoning time but tend to conceive of units of time, like minutes and hours or weeks and months, as independent temporal structures rather than as aspects of the same chronology. It is as though architects had to measure length in feet, width in meters and height in ells; as though basic instruction manuals demanded a knowledge of five different languages. It is no wonder then that we often look into our own immediate past or future, last Tuesday or a week from Sunday, with feelings of helpless confusion. Crucial elements of past and future, and indeed the encompassing coherence of time itself, are obscured from us by thickets of asymmetry.

XI.4 ✍ WHAT IF THIS LANGUAGE OF TIME could be reformed into one which would bring all chronological units, from the second on up to the year, into harmony with a single number system? Variations on this theme (now commonly known as "metric time") are at least as old as the late eighteenth century, when a calendar based on the decimal system was legislated by the French Revolution and retained in practice nationally for more than twelve years, from autumn of 1793 through 1805 (see pages 152–153 for an English abstract). Subdiurnal decimal reforms were considered but never initiated. What follows is a hypothetical example of a metric year and day:

> One year (about 365.25 days): 12 months of 30 days each + one holiday period of 5 to 6 days (variable for leap years).*
> One month: 30 days (= 3 weeks). Months would be renamed to suggest their position in the annual sequence.
> One week: 10 days (= 200 hours = 10,000 minutes = 1,000,000 seconds). 7-day work periods, 3-day weekends. Days renamed to suggest position in week.
> One day: 20 hours (= 0.10 week = 1,000 minutes = 100,000 seconds).
> One decand: 2 hours (= 0.10 day). This would be a new unit of measurement, potentially valuable in calculations.
> One hour: 50 minutes (= 5,000 seconds = 1.2 hours of old notation).
> One minute: 100 seconds (= 1/1,000 day = 1.44 old minutes).
> One second: 1/100 minute (= 1/5,000 hour = 1/10,000 decand = 1/100,000 day = 1/1,000,000 week = .864 old second).

Many of the advantages of such a method of notation should be obvious. Without losing accuracy, it makes units of time coherent among themselves and coherent with the dynamics of mind. Our present system of notation, like the game of chess, is a pattern of arbitrary complications and restraints. Ornateness of this kind makes chess fascinating. With time and space, however, simplicity and harmony should be the rule. Within natural limitations, our method of reckoning time should be as steady and homogeneous as

---

* The 5 to 6 day periods at the year's end could be devoted to some sensible and necessary activity, like delirious merriment.

CALENDAR OF THE FRENCH REPUBLIC

	AUTUMN			WINTER		
	VINTAGE	MIST	FROST	SNOW	RAIN	WIND
	1st Decade	1st Decade	1st Decade	1st Decade	1st Decade	1st Decade
Primedi	1	1	1	1	1	1
Duodi	2	2	2	2	2	2
Tridi	3	3	3	3	3	3
Quartidi	4	4	4	4	4	4
Quintidi	5	5	5	5	5	5
Sextidi	6	6	6	6	6	6
Septidi	7	7	7	7	7	7
Octidi	8	8	8	8	8	8
Nonidi	9	9	9	9	9	9
Decadi	10	10	10	10	10	10
	2nd Decade	2nd Decade	2nd Decade	2nd Decade	2nd Decade	2nd Decade
Primedi	11	11	11	11	11	11
Duodi	12	12	12	12	12	12
Tridi	13	13	13	13	13	13
Quartidi	14	14	14	14	14	14
Quintidi	15	15	15	15	15	15
Sextidi	16	16	16	16	16	16
Septidi	17	17	17	17	17	17
Octidi	18	18	18	18	18	18
Nonidi	19	19	19	19	19	19
Decadi	20	20	20	20	20	20
	3rd Decade	3rd Decade	3rd Decade	3rd Decade	3rd Decade	3rd Decade
Primedi	21	21	21	21	21	21
Duodi	22	22	22	22	22	22
Tridi	23	23	23	23	23	23
Quintidi	24	24	24	24	24	24
Quartidi	25	25	25	25	25	25
Sextidi	26	26	26	26	26	26
Septidi	27	27	27	27	27	27
Octidi	28	28	28	28	28	28
Nonidi	29	29	29	29	29	29
Decadi	30	30	30	30	30	30

CALENDAR OF THE FRENCH REPUBLIC

SPRING			SUMMER		
BUD	BLOSSOM	MEADOW	HARVEST	HEAT	FRUIT
1st Decade	1st Decade	1st Decade	1st Decade	1st Decade	1st Decade
1	1	1	1	1	1
2	2	2	2	2	2
3	3	3	3	3	3
4	4	4	4	4	4
5	5	5	5	5	5
6	6	6	6	6	6
7	7	7	7	7	7
8	8	8	8	8	8
9	9	9	9	9	9
10	10	10	10	10	10
2nd Decade	2nd Decade	2nd Decade	2nd Decade	2nd Decade	2nd Decade
11	11	11	11	11	11
12	12	12	12	12	12
13	13	13	13	13	13
14	14	14	14	14	14
15	15	15	15	15	15
16	16	16	16	16	16
17	17	17	17	17	17
18	18	18	18	18	18
19	19	19	19	19	19
20	20	20	20	20	20
3rd Decade	3rd Decade	3rd Decade	3rd Decade	3rd Decade	3rd Decade
21	21	21	21	21	21
22	22	22	22	22	22
23	23	23	23	23	23
24	24	24	24	24	24
25	25	25	25	25	25
26	26	26	26	26	26
27	27	27	27	27	27
28	28	28	28	28	28
29	29	29	29	29	29
30	30	30	30	30	30

Republican Days

Primedi	1
Duodi	2
Tridi	3
Quartidi	4
Quintidi	5

time itself, and should reflect the rhythm and pulse of natural things. A metric system would turn the clouded glass through which we normally view time into something like clear crystal. It would make us abler to understand time's challenges, to use time well.

XI.5 ✍ SOME LESS OBVIOUS ADVANTAGES OF THE metric system:

The total number of days in the "working" year, 360, is one of the two most arithmetically "abundant" and useful numbers in its order of magnitude (exceeded in this only by its multiple, 720). It is divisible by every number from 1 to 10 except the notorious 7. It is the number of degrees in a circle, the number of points on a compass. It is one short of being a perfect square.

Because 30 is divisible by 10, each month would begin on the same day of the week; and every date in the month would be permanently associated with a single weekday. These relationships would be easy to memorize. Because of this factor and the dominance of the decimal system in the new calendar, there would no longer be any difficulty in looking forward or backward to determine days or dates. The week-month dichotomy, and the difficulty in reckoning from month to month, would be completely alleviated.

Children would be introduced to time as something transparently and classically simple, indivisible from number and simple logic, cognate with music, architecture, natural symmetry and moral principle.

Because the year would contain sixteen fewer weekends, there would be proportionally fewer Mondays and Fridays (or whatever they would be called) — fewer disoriented and wasteful beginnings and ends of work weeks. People working seven-day stretches would be able to gain more momentum, coherence and communication during their periods of effort, which would be 40 percent longer.

Critics who oppose this idea because it prescribes apparent marathons of work should remember that, all else being equal, leisure is not intrinsically more pleasurable than work, and that both leisure and work can be improved by being made more temporally coherent.

XI.6 ✍️   I HAVE STRUCTURED THIS BOOK ON THE French Republican calendar: (1) partly because my method of composition, profuse and discontinuous, did not allow of anything more organic than a long sequence of short passages, and I could not find a better way than this to give them a kind of order; (2) partly because I wish the book to suggest a kind of circularity rather than a specific beginning and end; and (3) partly in order to represent, through the number and variety of these writings, the immense and miscellaneous volume of a single year of life.

XI.7 ✍️   THE NORMAL WRISTWATCH (OLD STYLE) has three hands, and although these three take the same course over the same field of vision, we distinguish automatically between the amounts of time they measure. Equally automatically our minds adjust to the particular dimensions of a given time scale; as, for example, 60 seconds is a long time to hold an isometric posture; 60 minutes is a long time to write without resting; 12 hours is a long time to go without food or drink. We also move and think in grander time scales, equally distinct from each other, equally capable of eliciting automatic responses. One hand on our mental clock rotates once a week, another once a month, another with the seasons, another with the years. Yet another concerns our position in various stages of life: childhood, youth, middle age, etc. Set within the immense expanse of time which is a human life, these eight orders of magnitude themselves differ so extremely in duration that we have trouble comparing one with another or thinking of two simultaneously; instead we tend to approach each one with a different, exclusive sort of awareness. In order to think coherently about time, we must at some level of awareness unify these orders of magnitude, understand them as aspects of a single flow of great and small things, see that we move slowly with respect to the former, quickly with respect to the latter, but nonetheless within a single vast environment. This is perhaps our only way of approaching one of the most difficult problems we face in life: that of distinguishing between the temporary and the lasting things; between the truly urgent issues and the clamor of trifles. Without such an understanding we are disunified, fragmented personalities — unconscious hypocrites who apply different sets of values to different time scales, betraying the values of one scale when we focus on another.

XI.8 🖎 THE SEVEN-DAY WEEK, WITH ITS regularized periods of work and play, sets up a psychological rhythm which is shared by almost all of us. It is a little roller-coaster of highs and lows, fasts and slows, which gives immediate human meaning to the broader expanse of time but also distracts us from time's natural sequences and inexorable flow. At best it is a social contract or necessary compromise between the needs of society and those of the individual. It sustains moderate activity without submerging either side; it keeps the system going and rewards our labor with rest and the tribal comforts of ritual. At worst it is a subtle emotional tyranny under whose power we abandon all hope of real freedom and instead engage in a petty charade of human significance, the endless rerun of a cheap comedy which we pathetically identify with our own progress and growth. The metronomic alternation between work and nonwork implants in us misleading distinctions between these two modalities, leading us to associate work with unpleasant subjection and nonwork with liberated pleasure. Because we work arbitrary amounts of time, we tend to conceive of work in terms of time rather than in terms of accomplishment. Because work has temporal structure, we unconsciously associate leisure with temporal disorganization. And over this deadening rhythm is played, again and again, the same psychological bolero: Monday, the Day of Wrath; Tuesday and Wednesday, the grind; weary Thursday, across whose fallowness Friday, a prostitute-goddess of inexplicably renewable freshness, beckons with a promise of unspecified fulfillment. This promise is based on the lie that human nature, unfulfilled by work, can be fulfilled by leisure. Of course the promise is never kept; we spend Saturday and Sunday consecrating the week's successes and failures to oblivion, in deepening dread of the Monday to come.

XI.9 🖎 ARE THERE FEASIBLE ALTERNATIVES to this routine? Here, as elsewhere, the recognition of our subjugation is the first step. Awareness of the ultimate goal of work, in terms of development, achievement and social value, and awareness of the common bonds which link work with leisure, are further steps. More comprehensive solutions depend on individual circumstance and experience. In my own academic profession, where institutionalized poverty is compensated for by the freedom to organize one's days, I have worked my way through a number of anomalous time systems. A few years ago, when my livelihood depended on the satisfactory completion of a book, I (lectures and meetings excepted) forgot the week altogether and lived through whole seasons, term in term out, for the three or four hours per day I could give to writing. Later, while I worked on this book in California, the final arbiter of my time was a young babysitter. If she took Wednesday off, I did not write on Wednesday; when she worked all week, so did I. This year I teach on Tuesdays and Thursdays. The seven-day week has meaning for me only as the container for a special "two-week" system: a T–W–T university week and an F–S–S–M writing week. These miniweeks are distinct time periods for me and have their own beginnings, middles and ends. Monday morning, Friday evening and the weekends hold little importance for me at all; the dramatic times are Thursday evening and Tuesday morning. You may object that this last system is but an intensification of the conventional system I have just attacked; and I must admit that, working two weeks in one, I seem to be aging rather faster than usual. But the difference (as attested to by the lack of a "leisure" period) is that I enjoy what I am doing: that my time, as an expression of what I think important in life, is my own. Indeed, I might think that I held an enviable place in time, if it were not for the example of my young children, who exhaust the gamut of experience in a single day and find every minute some new woe or wonder.

XI.10 ⚶ OUR COMMON METHODS OF NOTING the passage of time in calendars and using calendars as means of time management generally reflect the weakness and confusion of our temporal awareness. Calendars that show a given month arranged in weeks on a single large page, or those that include one to seven days on successive pages, do little more than synchronize us with the rest of society. They can help us plan our work in advance; they can save us from showing up in a distant and empty meeting hall on the evening of Mr. Diddlezeit's cocktail party; but branded like us with the curse of routine, they can neither tell us anything new about time nor teach us to find our freedom in it. We cannot do without these devices, which in a manner of speaking help us pay what we owe to Caesar; but there is no reason why we cannot keep one calendar for Caesar and another for ourselves. At best this subversive calendar should ignore the usual pattern of weeks and months, reflecting instead the homogeneous and coherent flow of time, the natural similarity of one day to another. They should be organized decimally, for we count and calculate in 10's and multiples of 10. Leaving schedules and obligations to the conventional calendar, we should consecrate our own to a more internal dynamics: to essential outlays of vital energy — our growth, achievement, pleasure and love. We should project these activities forward, in lines or bands, as indispensable components of future time, forming together a substratum of humanity without which all other action is meaningless. And also we should note our success or failure in experiencing them. For this calendar, as guide to present action and projection of will into the future, is incomplete unless it can also serve as a measure and reminder of the past.

XI.11 ✒ TAKING A LIFE SPAN OF SEVENTY-FIVE years as one limit of measurement and a single second as the other, our mean unit of time — that is, a period as much longer than a second as it is shorter than a life span — is about 13.5 hours, or roughly the period of a waking day. We have, in other words, about as many of these periods in each lifetime as we have seconds in each period: about 48,600 of each. By a strange coincidence, the waking day is by all odds the most "natural" period in human time: the period at once fullest of conscious and unconscious significance and most subject to our shaping will. Indeed, in much the same way that a single person might choose a modest ranch house, or a solitary fisherman a trim cabin cruiser, the waking day is the human vessel of time, the unit which, more than any other, seems roomy, manageable and secure. But beyond this unit, both to the side of great and the side of little, our minds tend to swim. How can we direct ourselves wisely through weeks and months when sleep and night, like overzealous janitors, sweep away yesterday's discoveries and muddle tomorrow's resolve? And how can we reckon with the tens of thousands of daily seconds which, if apprehended singly, would belabor us to death with a sense of our own missed opportunities and vain pretenses? We cling desperately to the standard of day, a flag of gold edged on each side with black — powerless at once to dominate the longer flow of time and to appreciate the hidden vastness of meaning within.

XI.12 ⚐ A WELL-KNOWN AUTHOR WAS ONCE asked to talk to a group of grammar school children about the art of writing. Instead of speaking to them about inspiration, self-discipline, esthetic theory and other abstractions, he concentrated surprisingly on the physical aspects of his work. Simply but with much detail he described his study, its lighting, his desk; he showed them the pads and pencils he used; he spoke of when and for how long he did his writing each day. The children were fascinated. In all likelihood they had never before been offered such a vivid connection between their own and the adult world. What the author had done was appeal to their own universal and instinctive delight for the materials of work. He knew that their own implements — the pads, fresh blackboards, pristine boxed chalk and delectable white paste — were wonderful to the children not only in themselves but as the immediate vehicles of expression and achievement. He was aware of this because, as an independent writer, free to organize his own time and space, he was still susceptible to the same wonder and delight. But for most of us others this is mere nostalgia. Our working environments, which exert compelling influences on our performance, are foisted on us by corporate purveyors whose imaginations do not extend beyond the common denominators of drudgery. When budgets allow, they are decked out with carpets, random padding and generally useless space. We treat them much the way taxi drivers treat their cabs. Whenever possible, we ignore them; and, in that this voluntary oblivion constitutes a loss of touch with our environment, it is worse for us than positive distaste. Equally degraded is our time, which, depending on our role in life, is mangled and scrambled in a variety of ways. Like one of those

huge offices, separated into roofless and doorless cubicles for dozens of clerks or sales representatives, our time is broken up in such
a way as to give us neither undisturbed solitude nor relaxed com-
munion with others. The worst agent of this confusion is the telephone, whose ringing is almost never planned or expected, and
whose mere silent presence (like some horrible radio that can turn
itself on at its own whim) has a disunifying effect on our awareness. Add to this the commutation, the allegedly refreshing "breaks,"
the epidemic proliferation of media, the increasingly large number
of things which each year we are told that we ought to do, enjoy,
fear or possess, and our general ignorance of the value of open
time, and you will no longer wonder why we are lazy, distressed
and unproductive, both as individuals and as nations.

XI.13 ✒ OFFICE MANAGERS SHOULD CONSIDER
(unless necessity dictates otherwise) assuring their executive staffs
of one hour per day when they will not be disturbed by calls or
visits. Ideally this should be the hour just before they leave work.
This will allow them to put the day's concerns in order and to plan,
reasonably and with a clear desk, for the next day's work.

XI.14 ✒ THE SCHOOLBOY LEARNS QUICKLY TO
divide his day into periods which he does or does not enjoy. He
may enjoy meeting his friends as he walks to school, his lunch and
play period, the final bell, his homecoming and subsequent bursting
out of doors; and not enjoy rising from bed, brushing his teeth, entering the schoolhouse, selected subjects, and going to bed. He
lives a mixed day, but an ordered one; and even with his youthfully
expansive sense of time he need not look too far ahead without perceiving some future pleasure. But adults are often deprived of this
solace. Young mothers, for example, live in a disorganized variety
of unexpected pains and pleasures and are thus incapable of enjoying the future or indulging themselves in the present. Housewives
without children are often little better off. These poor people, and
all of us who are dissatisfied with our time, might do better by trying to regularize a few pleasant experiences during the day, fixing

them in time and thus stabilizing our awareness through them. In-dividual activities aside, the mere act of planning one's day with this goal in mind will be an important personal victory.

XI.15 🖋 THE HAPPY INDIVIDUAL IS ABLE TO renew daily and with full consciousness all the basic expressions of human identity: work, love, communication, play and rest.

XI.16 🖋 A CONCERT PIANIST GIVES A PERFORMANCE which wins acclaim and earns money. The money feeds and rests and houses him and gives him time to practice for his next con-cert, which, all else being equal, will win more acclaim and earn more money. Which of these activities and commodities is a means, and which an end? What we see, first of all, is a regular and inte-gral sequence in which each element is at once desirable in itself and necessary for some further step. Nothing in this sequence can be dismissed as drudgery or, conversely, raised to the position of a final cause. Such a life is analogous to cyclical operations in the natural world and in direct contrast to the lives of most other peo-ple, who distinguish so sharply between means and ends that much of their life is spent in imperfect commitment and despised as rou-tine. Moreover, if we asked this pianist which element of his life was, if not the end and goal, at least the most pleasurable, he would be likely to answer that it was the performance itself. Here the contrast between his life and others would be most extreme. For if we look at the pianist's art in terms of the theory of work in gen-eral, the act of performance is precisely equivalent to the *act of labor*, the paper-pusher's pushing of paper, the stone-breaker's breaking of stone, the varieties of strenuous engagement, full of boredom and fatigue and anxiety, which we tolerate solely because they earn us bread. This reversal of values, coupled with the obvious nobility of the pianist's life, can teach us something about the drawbacks of our own. It suggests that happiness consists not (as modern prac-tices imply) in the simplification and curtailment of work coupled with the amplification of leisure, but rather in work as a significant and humane activity. The elusive component of dignity and pleasure, which we bemoan as absent from modern life and tend to seek in countless fads and distractions, may well reside in labor itself.

XI.17 ✒ ON THIS SUBJECT IT IS STRIKING to note how many individuals pursue, outside of their own professions and with a kind of rebellious delight, hobbies that are no more than personalized forms of work. This suggests that one of the hidden desires of humanity, provoked by the inward clamor of unused potentialities, is the dream of work in freedom.

XI.18 ✒ THOSE WHO LABOR FOR BREAD OR money alone are condemned to their reward.

XI.19 ✒ THE TYPICAL LARGE CORPORATION has one department for the generating of ideas and other departments for the application of them. Thus the corporate system discourages genuine creativity, which demands the challenge of both forms of activity.

XI.20 ✒ MODERN GOVERNMENTS WOULD DO well to encourage corporations, *via* large tax credits, to build decent residences for their workers on or near the business property. If it became widespread, this practice would result in significant energy savings, increased economic activity (in construction, sales and services), greater traffic safety and convenience and, no less importantly, enhanced human time. Workers, moreover, would save a good deal of the money normally spent on cars, fuel and/or mass transit. It may be objected that this plan would dehumanize society by substituting, for our normal miscellaneous liberties, the colorless stereotype of life in a work colony. But actual comparisons (for example, between farming communities in Israel and their counterparts in the Soviet Union), as well as common sense, suggest that it is the quality of involvement rather than the general sort of organization which distinguishes a "human" setting from one which is not. Quite probably the greater number of blue-collar workers would find life in such a community (if its potential for safety, convenience, economy and beauty were fulfilled) superior in human terms to what they have now and must look forward to in the future. The most basic conditions obtaining in such a community — the cooperative ownership of services, the proximity and safety of schools, the walk to and from work without loading oneself into a conveyance or crossing a major street — would be sources of pleasure.

Conversely, corporations which build factories far from actual or potential residential areas, and cities whose zoning laws necessitate this practice, should be docked sharply as perpetrators of fatigue and waste.

XI.21 ⚞ LAZINESS — THE PURE FEAR AND SIMPLE loathing of work — almost never appears except in some disguise; and of all its disguises, the most effective and prevalent is that of miscellaneous activity. We sit down early at our desk, shuffle papers from one side of it to another, muse distractedly, check our scalp for potential itches, and look at the clock for no reason at all. We get up and, with a look of singular care and intelligence, sharpen our pencils. Back at our desk, we arrange the day's priorities. We begin Item 1 but cannot get our mind off Item 2, a long-neglected issue which opens channels of such profound guilt that, in pure self-defense, we make an irrelevant phone call. The call, which begins in a businesslike vein, broadens and inflates into an inquiry which touches urbanely on the prime interest rate, personal medical history and the comparative excellence of delicatessens. We hang up and wonder where we were, begin a letter while trying to remember, and decide that it is time for coffee. At coffee we attempt with much success to obliterate all concerns from our mind. Afterward we return to our desk and Item 1 but, having left our door open for fresh air, we are dropped in on by a friend. This friend habitually practices another covert form of laziness: he is a marathon talker. His arsenal of diversions includes office gossip, knowledgeable inquiries about our family, current fads, processible slanders about successful men and women, and appeals for sympathy. We listen to him submissively, partners in a conspiracy against work which, in order to be shared successfully, must remain unacknowledged. Twenty minutes are killed for all time. He flees guiltily at the sound of our phone. We answer, pleased at the new distraction, but find to our horror that it is a self-righteous villain asking us what the hell has happened to Item 2. We reply with hollow earnestness that we have been extremely busy. He reproaches us with impending dates and places. We hang up, set Item 2 squarely in the middle of our desk, and discover that it is time for lunch. At lunch a passing colleague asks us how we are. We look up with a martyred smile. "Harried, as usual."

XI.22 ✍ WE STRUGGLE WITH, AGONIZE OVER AND bluster heroically about the great questions of life when the answers to most of these lie hidden in our attitude toward the thousand minor details of each day.

XI.23 ✍ REGRETTING WASTED TIME IS ITSELF A waste of time, an unconscious strategy of evasion.

XI.24 ✍ LARGE PORTIONS OF EACH DAY — ESPECIALLY those devoted to some form of subordinate routine — are regularly thrown upon the junk heap of time. Dismissing these periods as inconsequential, or using the classic evasion that they are only means to an end, we tend to pass them in immemorable and unrefreshing distraction. Yet these periods, taken in gross, are by no means short or insignificant, and used well they can contribute to the healthy rhythm of the day.

In an average lifetime, one spends (by my reckoning) about 1½ years at breakfast, eight months in the shower and an equal period on the toilet. The commuter who lives 30 minutes from work is well over a year in transit. The housewife devotes about two years to cooking. Workers take a year for lunch, and six months for their coffee breaks. How can these unprepossessing activities be improved? By remembering, I submit, a few rules which apply to time in general. Time is best spent when we are

1. Concentrating wholly on what we are doing
2. Freeing our minds from thought altogether
3. Communicating honestly with others
4. Dreaming asleep or awake
5. Planning
6. Remembering.

The cook can labor not just to prepare food but to prepare it well. The toothbrusher can (because his activity is automatic) relax his mind altogether; or he can free it from the diurnal jumble of thoughts by devoting his full awareness to the extirpation of nasty food particles. The person on the toilet, who probably cannot (as Rabelais' Gargantua could) employ a tutor to enhance this necessary activity by explaining "obscure and difficult" sections of the Holy Writ, can instead meditate, daydream or think coherently about the operation of his own body. Breakfast, coffee breaks and lunch can, with small effort, become periods of valuable communication. Commuters can converse, sleep, plan, daydream, read, or, if they are driving, think about what they are passing, when and why. All these are valid and renewing occupations. What is to be avoided is preoccupation and disordered occupation — the compulsive worry, the nervous escape from thought to thought, the scratching and hair-fluffing, the short circuit of distraction.

XI.25 🙋 WE ARE NOT GREAT CONNOISSEURS of the two twilights. We miss the dawning, exclusably enough, by sleeping through it, and are as much strangers to the shadowless welling-up of day as to the hesitant return of consciousness in our slowly waking selves. But our obliviousness to evening twilight is less understandable. Why do we almost daily ignore a spectacle (and I do not mean sunset but rather the hour, more or less, afterward) that has a thousand tonalities, that alters and extends reality, that offers, more beautifully than anything man-made, a visual metaphor of peace? To say that it catches us at busy or tired moments won't do; for in temperate latitudes it varies by hours from solstice to solstice. Instead I suspect that we shun evening twilight because it offers two things which, as insecurely rational beings, we would rather not appreciate: the vision of irrevocable cosmic change (indeed, change into darkness), and a sense of deep ambiguity — of objects seeming to be more, less, other than we think them to be. We are noontime and midnight people, and such devoted camp-followers of certainty that we cannot endure seeing it mocked and undermined by nature.

There is a brief period of twilight of which I am especially fond, little more than a moment, when I see what seems to be color without light, followed by another brief period of light without color. The earlier period, like a dawn of night, calls up such sights as at all other times are hidden, wistful half-formless presences neither of day nor night, that draw up with them similar presences in the mind.

XI.26 ⚐ SOCIOBIOLOGISTS ARGUE THAT THE MIND is a machine whose primary purpose is to protect the genes, and that all our claims to freedom of thought must be qualified by this physiological consideration. In order to see that this theory is highly improbable, we need only look at recent research in a more elemental branch of science, molecular biology. Here it is currently seen as probable that one of the most extreme changes in natural history, the development from chemical activity to biological activity, occurred on earth without external intervention, through casual chemical interactions nurtured by benign circumstances, enormous numbers of chances and huge amounts of time. If such an immense alteration in the quality of phenomena can occur in unmotivated nature, why cannot we assume the possibility of a much less awesome change — that from mechanistic impulse to free will — in the more than ten billion cells of the human brain, encouraged by necessity, time, pleasure and the development of contemplative and communicative abilities?

That sociobiology should be quite attractive to many humanists and social scientists is not at all surprising, for large elements of these professions have been trying for quite a while to abdicate human freedom. That natural scientists should find it convincing is much less likely; for modern natural science has opened up a world which, far from being monodirectional or mechanistic, is full of dynamism, elegance, astonishment and poetic beauty.

XI.27 ✍ OUR WILDERNESS IN CARMEL VALLEY boasted a legion of earwigs, a large dog-chasing doe and a number of black widow spiders. My wife found the first of the black widows one day in June and managed to take it alive in a small jar. The size and markings were unmistakable — an impressively large black creature with an orange-red hourglass on the underside of its abdomen. I forced air-holes in the lid of the jar. The spider crouched at the base of the jar in an attitude suggesting caution and patience. Unlike a more terrible-looking eight-legged creature (a solpugid) caught a week earlier, it did not assume menacing postures and try to escape. It merely waited. My plan was to drown it in water, pickle it in gin and keep it as an admonitory specimen; but I delayed. I returned the next day, expecting to discover the usual signs of fatigue and despair (the solpugid had been comatose after one day and soon expired); but instead I found something remarkably different. Using the longest internal dimension of the jar — the diagonal between one side of the lid and the other side of the base — the spider had built a rich and complex web. This was surprising, because of the several other large spiders I had captured in jars (one does these things in California), none had made an effort to take up housekeeping, and also because, as arachnologists tell us, distressed spiders tend to build ineffective and ugly webs. Besides, with the solpugid in recent memory, I could not help wondering why the same circumstances which drove one creature into a frenzy could leave another so philosophical and unperturbed. Obviously the black widow, through mere natural reflex, had taken notice of the fact that it was endangered, exiled from its habitat, sterilely imprisoned. Nature does not allow of the stupidity which ignores danger or the arrogance which disregards it. I had to assume that the spider, naturally alert to her straitened circumstances, had by some more subtle natural reflex determined to make the best of them; that, cognizant of her prison's disheartening lack of airborne traffic, she had nonetheless prepared for the unlikely windfall which would allow her to continue her existence. The next day I drowned the spider. As the tap water rose and covered her she again refused to struggle, as though realizing that the longer she saved her inhaled air, the more chance there was that some new turn of events, some new variation of the demonstrably unpredictable cosmos, might save her life.

XI.28 ✍ I SUGGESTED EARLIER (1.16) THAT ONE way of thinking about time's dimensionality was through comparisons like that between a pebble (small spatially but large temporally) and a cloud (large spatially but small temporally). With this concept in mind, we may look at a more difficult issue: the comparative spatial and temporal dimensionality of human experience. We may compare, for example, the human being with the dimensions of the space-time continuum itself. By current reckoning, the universe has a radius of 20 billion light-years (a light-year is about 6 trillion miles) and consequently a known age of 20 billion years. Divide your approximate height into the radius of the universe. Then divide your age into the age of the universe. No matter what your height and age, you will find that you are immensely larger in time than you are in space. If your size in time were as small as your size in space, you would live less than one-millionth of a second. If your size in space were as large as your size in time, you would need a microscope to examine the solar system. Pygmies in space, we are bumbling giants in time.

XI.29 ✍ WHILE THE SPACE-TIME CONTINUUM IS currently the playing field of physicists, its psychological implications have gone virtually unexplored. In 1.17, I discussed the possibility of a four-dimensional symmetry, an esthetic equipoise of the spatial and the temporal. Examples of this phenomenon are legion. We are all disappointed when soap bubbles break too quickly, and would be equally deprived of joy if we could keep them in the cupboard or whack them around like golf balls. They are pleasing not through shape or duration but through a unique relationship between the two. A chord of music, a shared glance, a handshake or a kiss loses significance if it is ended too quickly or held too long. Are such shared values merely conventions, common patterns of human sensation which have no analogies in the natural world? Or can it be said that such ephemera are hints of a truly unified being, windows to the joy and order which animate nature and often seem to mock humanity. We should at least consider the possibility, suggested so forcibly by physics, that time is not merely an attribute of being but rather its pith and substance.

XI.30 🔏 VACATIONING. TYPICAL SUNNY DAY AT a lake in Mendocino County, California, September 1979:

7 to 10 A.M.: Laze in bed as sun flickers through red curtains
10 to 11 A.M.: swim in lake and eat large, fat breakfast
11 A.M. to 1 P.M.: sit writing in wicker chair under locust tree
1 to 3:30 P.M.: brief swims, sunning half-asleep afloat on rubber raft
3:30 to 5 P.M.: excursion with family into the woods
5 to 5:30 P.M.: run, or swim across the lake, for exercise
5:30 to 8 P.M.: making fire, cocktails, putting children to sleep
8 to 10 P.M.: dinner
10 P.M. to midnight: reading.

Close to perfect days, not only because everything in them is pleasant but also because of the large dimensions of time, time opening up spatially into vistas of clear hours; and in the greater distance, banks of clear days opening up both past and future. Activities which seem endless because they will be repeated and because each is indulged to its natural fullness. It is not enough merely to recapture time; like a princess once hostage, she must be restored to her early dignities.

XII ⚜ MEMORY

XII.1 ⚜ OF ALL OUR MENTAL FACULTIES, MEMORY is the most underestimated, most misused. That creative resource which Plato called the key to elemental truth is set to menial chores; that free selectivity among an almost infinite treasury of sensation lies neglected. Lacking coherence with our own past we frequently feel marooned in present time. Lacking a continuum of identity we are compelled, by daily challenges, to reinvent ourselves on the spot. This offense against memory would be shameful enough if it were merely due to laziness; but it is also due to something darker: a terror of self-knowledge as quiet and subtle as our terror of the unconscious.

XII.2 ⚜ TO HONOR MEMORY WE MUST FREE IT, disorder its arbitrary compartments, disengage it whenever possible from practical necessity. Rather than consult it, we must listen for it. It will tell us unequivocally what matters. Years ago I passed the high wall of a schoolyard and heard great shouts inside. A soccer ball rose into the bright sunlight above the wall and fell back. Remembering that moment ever since then I have thought of vicarious pleasure, pleasure divorced from self and object, pleasure of brightness and motion.

XII.3 ⚜ THE COMPARTMENTALIZATION OF MEMORY can be a subtle and casuistic tool of the defensive ego. We can file, for example, the assorted offenses of others against us in one part of our memory, and our assorted offenses against others in another part. The former chamber of awareness is likely to be large, well-lit and easily accessible to many other rooms and corridors; the latter chamber is likely to be dark and remote, available only through a single sequence of difficult and painful turnings. It takes great will-power and even enlightened intelligence for us to be able to compare the contents of these two chambers and admit their bearing upon each other. Failing this unlikely revelation, we become apprenticed to hypocrisy.

XII.4 ⚑ WE CONSULT TROOPS OF SPECIALISTS ON the question of how to live, when memory alone, heard with common sense and compassion, will tell us most of what we need to know.

XII.5 ⚑ INSCRIBED IN LARGE LETTERS ON the floor at the entrance to Westminister Abbey is a single phrase, "REMEMBER WINSTON CHURCHILL." The implication is not that this statesman is likely to be forgotten. It is rather that his enduring political characteristics — that blend of magnanimity, vigilance and pure outrage which made him Hitler's most effective enemy — are qualities little prized by liberal democracies and soon forgotten by nations at peace. A primary function of memory is that of warning us, not merely against the repetition of our own error and excesses, but also against vulnerability to the error and excess of others. If our minds held a parliament, our wills would be liberal, our memories conservative.

XII.6 ⚑ EXPERIENCE MERELY FORGOTTEN IS seldom beyond recall, if we try hard and patiently to bring it back. It is only when we forget having forgotten that a door closes between us and the past.

XII.7 ✍ PROUST, WHO RIGHTLY SAW MEMORY AS the indispensable function of human identity, made much of the fact that a single accidental phenomenon, striking the proper chord, could open up whole avenues of an individual's forgotten emotional past. Similarly, when we strive to reconstruct some period deep in our own past, it is helpful to search for some physical detail which is remembered almost viscerally and which, when felt again, may bring with it the whole emotional context of earlier time. The winter of my first year at college was full of miscellaneous experiences; but the key to all of them is the simple feeling of icy air on my face — the sudden blast that would hit us as, ruffled in overcoats, we strode out of our dorm at night in search of adventure. Significantly, this feeling is not only the psychological key opening up a whole complex of experiences, but also a poetic symbol for the combined effect — one of brisk and perilous excitement — which these experiences had on me. This duality of code and symbol also operates in Proust. His most striking memory code (in *Combray*) is a dried flower which, steeped in hot water for tea, swells and opens again to resemble its former being. This flower operates as (1) a key by which the hero recovers his own past, (2) a symbol of the reinstatement of lost identity, and (3) a symbol of the power of art to awaken the communal memory and communal identity of its audience.

XII.8 ✍ FREQUENTLY AND WITH DELIBERATION and respect we should revisit our early memories — memories which do not fade and which hold the incorruptible essence of emotion. These memories are the parts of us which change least with time, perhaps because they come from periods when we were most in tune with time; and coming back to them we come upon ourselves — not the harried, hustling, temporary selves we see when we compromise with the mirror, but rather what Yeats called "the pilgrim soul," at once most our own and most confluent with the race.

XII.9 ✍ MY EARLIEST CONSCIOUS MEMORY IS THE sight, from a supine position in my baby carriage, of broken white clouds against a blue sky; and that one memory carries with it the full force of a happy infancy. Other times an unusual assortment of details, bonded indivisibly in memory, will unlock emotions unique and almost magical. When I was three years old, I lived with my parents in a rented carriage house on a large estate in Rumson, New Jersey. The house was next to a duck pond in a forest. On one side of the forest were fenced pastures; on the other were lawns leading to the main house. On the verge of the forest facing the lawns was a small screened structure with a full-sized wooden horse in it. My mother would walk me to this little house and set me on the horse's back, and I would sit contentedly in the shady house of screens facing the sunny lawns. To this day I have no idea what the house and horse were for, and oddly enough it was over thirty years before I even asked myself this question. As a child of three, I had no idea of purpose; things existed in and for themselves. A large wooden horse in a lonely screened house had as full and comprehensive a being as a home or a car or a duck pond. And even now that memory brings me a partial sense of that poetic fullness, a ghostly residue of unqualified being.

XII.10 ✠ MY WIFE AND I SPENT THE FALL OF 1968 renting an old farmhouse in the Tuscan hills. During the first couple of weeks there, I was taken with an unexpected zeal to write and began the first draft of a novel. Our daily life during those months was an image of peace and pleasure. We would rise early and consume strong coffee, unsalted bread and a cheese something like hard jack on the always sunny porch. Then for four or five hours we would each retire, she to her studies, I to my writing. In the afternoon we would shop in the village, or drive to some near-by town, or write letters or visit with neighbors. Later I would start a fire for the bath and then go jogging on trails over hills covered with oak and broom or along rocky roads through Chianti vineyards and olive groves. The daytime air was warm and dry, and the evenings had a winter freshness. Our bath was enjoyed to the rumbling and crackling of the wood water heater. We had long cocktails on the porch, drinking a mixture of Italian gin and Italian tonic that tasted like a kind of cold juniper tea. We gave the whole evening to dinner and sitting by the fire in the big hearth. Other periods in my life leave vague images in my memory; even if lengthier and more recent than Italy, they are vague, disorganized and incomplete. But the Italian days, like a dream unequivocally realized, are clear as well water, a full and immediate evocation. They give comfort during less delightful times and are in fact a kind of monument of identity — not our individual identity so much as our possible and once-realized humanness. My wife said that they are like beautiful pictures hung on the wall of consciousness, always available to refresh and challenge present time.

XII.11 🖎 EUGENE, OREGON. WE HAVE NOW BEEN out of our rented house in Carmel Valley for almost two months; for almost as long, another family have been renting it and making it their own. The various rooms and outdoor areas I habitually used for half a year — physical contexts which became, comfortably and pleasantly, extensions of my own identity — slip out of mind now; especially since, on returning to Eugene, I assumed like some mental garment the physical context of the house we own. And with these passing memories I lose a treasure, or at least the key to one: an intricate web of symbol and detail which, like a genetic code, can unlock and revive the happiness of time past. I have no sense of feeling orphaned from the Carmel Valley house. In fact, like many other twentieth-century types, I travel often and quickly feel at ease in new surroundings. But this very adaptability may constitute the real loss. For am I not defending myself against the past, playing false to it — trashing fickly, as something of no value at all, the few effective manifestations of prior identity? Our modern haste to adapt, to conform to the variable present, involves a quietly destructive attitude toward the past and toward our sense of self.

XII.12 🖎 IT IS 10:15 ON A SUNNY MAY MORNING. I am working in the spare room, listening to our babysitter Amie give her usual morning concert to Anthony in the living room next door. Amie sings well, accompanies herself on the guitar, and knows many songs. Anthony sometimes listens, sometimes sings, improvising his own words in good rhythm and a variety of atonal pitches. The sounds make me happy and help me write. What will this whole phenomenon, stretched out and repeated over weeks of mornings, become in memory? Probably a single monumental morning, a whole sense of morning and work and pleasure, a signet of calm and lingering time, a single song.

XII.13 ✒ THE HERO OF LAMPEDUSA'S *The Leopard* owns a huge old palace and claims grandly at one point that it must be a bore to know all the rooms of one's own house. Since in literature the house is often used as a metaphor for the mind, this remark implies that there are areas in our memory and/or imagination which are and should remain remote and mysterious. In *The Leopard*, the distant chambers of the hero's palace suggest illicit sexuality — walls hung anciently with chains and scourges, dusty beds inviting clandestine adventures. Thus we may infer a link between these exotic and unfamiliar rooms and the Freudian unconscious; we sense a connection between the parts of ourselves we seldom see and the psychological themes which embarrass or frighten us. To visit these rooms too often would be to undo the balance which keeps us sane; to visit them too seldom would be to deny the truth. Good psychiatrists, and artists like Lampedusa, lead us gracefully and harmlessly to their thresholds.

XII.14 ✒ IF TIME AND SPACE ARE ONE, IT FOLLOWS that those of us who possess more space must necessarily possess more time. This apparently absurd statement makes sense if we interpret "space" not as physical or physiological substance but rather as the extent of willed action. I would submit that the individual who extends his serious interests into broad areas of life, and his sympathy into the lives of others, is more conversant with the full volume of time, whether past, present, or future, than the individual who steers a narrow course. In support of this theory I offer admittedly feeble evidence from my own professional life. During the busy years of my late thirties, I taught at a university and worked on a scholarly book. Though I was anything but depressed, my time seemed to be telescoping drastically: days passed without leaving a hint of individual identity, and weeks, qualitatively similar to each other, went by in a blur. Holidays, seasonal changes and even anniversaries took me by surprise and were forgotten almost as soon as they had passed. I lost perspective in time and was often unable to distinguish the events of one recent year from those of another. This period came to a close when I finished my book and went on a year-long sabbatical which included extensive travel, new projects, several emergencies, and many vivid contacts with family and friends. My memory of that year is physically distinct from my memory of the years which preceded and followed it: as if a hallway, not unpleasant but somewhat dim and narrow, had opened into a broad and brilliant gallery, at the end of which it continued. Not only is this gallery brighter, taller and wider than the hallway; it is also proportionally *longer*, occupying far more temporal space than the years which preceded it and, paradoxically, far more than the year which has followed it. I can think back to a hundred events in it, giving their dates and places; while the next year, when I returned to my normal work, is already blurred and contracted in memory. What accounts for this revolution? Faced with an unremitting variety of new experience, I temporarily grew aware of the profound extent of time, the latent vastness of the present. Unexpecting, even unwilling, I was pulled out into time; and when I recognized its true dimensions I staked my claim and moved freely in it.

XII.15 ‎ IN A TRULY SENSIBLE PERSON, MEMORY is not only connected with will but is a primary function of will. To commit something to memory is a moral act, an assertion of value which reflects not only on particular phenomena but on one's personal experience in general. Analogously, to recall a memory is, to a greater or lesser extent, to reintegrate one's personality, to fortify and enlarge present being with the strength of the continuum. But in general our relationship with our own memories is slack and involuntary. Experiences ingrain themselves in us almost casually, because of their emotional aptness or their uniqueness or urgency. They are stored away unceremoniously and, if not called up by chance in the near future, are flattened and decomposed by other layers of experience. Seeking to remember, we wind our way back to events which were once full of complex and delightful detail and find them gutted, like undersea hulks that have lost their contents, their shape and all but the most rudimentary distinctions of character. And with them we lose that much of ourselves, of our form and mass in time, of the treasure of experience which, though it may connect us with others, is ours alone to protect and bestow.

XII.16 ✍ IN THE HEAT OF ACTION, THE MERE ability to remember our principles, our goals and the specific reasoning behind the course we have taken is an element of courage. Memory is fear's first victim.

XII.17 ✍ FEW THINGS GROW OLD SO FAST, OR AT least sink so swiftly into the mute and buried past, as a bottle of prescription pills. It is not just the typed labels, which fade and blotch so quickly under their transparent tape that after a few months the bottle seems to have floated around at sea for years; more importantly it is the operation of memory, which has speedily and effectively submerged the medicine and our sick need for it in oblivion, filed them in the dead letters of the mind. One might ascribe this quick forgetting to some instinctive love of health, a life urge so intense that it blocks out the awareness of illness in the same way that the sunlight blocks out the dark void of outer space. But the real reason, I suspect, is less noble than this. If we really loved health and hated disease, we would study and remember our illnesses, not only for abundant practical reasons but also because the memory of disease makes mere health a luxurious pleasure. It is rather our hatred of pain — indeed, our speechless terror of it — that makes us such good forgetters. Like Coleridge's poor traveler, who does not turn his head, "Because he knows a frightful fiend / Doth close behind him tread," we look fixedly away from past suffering. But while the traveler was, at least, aware of his own fear, ours is so deeply internalized that it is less a feeling than an antifeeling, a numbness to large areas of the past. And this numbness extends, beyond disease, to other equally powerful and dangerous sources of pain, blinding us to their latent survival, disarming us against their recurrence, condemning us to ignore destructively the tragic and comic potentialities of our lives.

XII.18 🖎 THOUGH WE MIGHT REASONABLY EXPECT life's surprises to imprint themselves on memory, the reverse is often true. Most of us, for example, tend to forget jokes, even good ones, and witty comments, no matter how devastating. These inventions, which depend heavily on the element of surprise, exert little weight on the mind once the surprise is past. Moreover, the very catharsis and brief oblivion they bring us constitute the first step in our forgetting them; like good doctors, they free us of both the illness and the remedy. Surprise of a different order is latent in great art and philosophy. Here patterns of truth, at once profoundly apt and profoundly alien to our habitual modes of apprehension, stun and awe us with a force that seems wholly transfiguring. Yet shortly afterward we are dragged back, by habit, inertia or the routine necessities of social self-defense, to our sodden old ways. The liberation has been incomplete; we honor the masterpiece but forget the message. Memory will only retain what the mind controls. Surprise, when it comes from a domain of truth beyond the mind's ordinary precincts, will normally fade from memory.

XII.19 🖎 WE HAVE LIBRARIES ON WAR AND SIN, disease and disaster; but I do not know of a single major book about forgetting, which is perhaps the most prevalent cause of all these other ills. So great is our oblivion to the subject or contempt for it that we have not even a word in English for the complex of psychological elements which predisposes us to forgetting (the U.S. senator, Sam Ervin, called it the "forgettory"). We commonly view it as a form of error, an intrusion of chaos — as vacuum rather than being. But modern psychiatry teaches us differently; and no philosophy which asserts that individuals are free, willing and responsible can ignore the contention that forgetting is a distinct act of will. We characteristically forget what is difficult, painful or terrible. Children forget their traumatic experiences, married couples their squabbles, recovered patients their illnesses, revelers their hangovers, nations their wars. True to the simplest laws of mechanics, the mind seeks to minimize its outlays of energy: not only the objects of memory but the very process of remembering is avoided, whenever possible, as an unnecessary effort. By and large we pay for these lapses, repeating our errors (as in the famous adage) because we have forgotten them. But the small punishments, though we may be condemned to a series of them for life, are inadequate to inspire lasting reform; while the larger punishments develop so slowly that we cannot imagine what caused them, and pain us so deeply that we forget about them as soon as possible.

XII.20   A FOOLISH PERSON IS NOT ONLY OBLIVIOUS to the necessities of the future but unfriendly to his own past. His manifold and miscellaneous blunders are expunged from memory, attributed to external circumstance, or otherwise laundered clean of blame; failing this, he may repudiate his own past, like some locust skin, as something he had transcended or outgrown. He habitually seeks the new, regarding each superficial change as a means to final success and tranquility, unaware that the same error can be made in a thousand different ways. He is so shallow in time, so oblivious to continuity, that the present itself, no matter how hackneyed or repetitious it may be, has always a glimmering newness for him, a promise of unprecedented and undeserved freedom. Each embrace of this promise is a rejection of true freedom, which is born of self-awareness and partakes as much of recollection as it does of planning. And contempt for one's past is a deadly form of self-contempt, an involuntary avowal of worthlessness which poisons every enterprise.

XII.21   IN DEALING WITH ANOTHER PERSON, try to carry the whole individual — his continuity from past through present to future — in your awareness. This way you will avoid both impulsive vituperations and cowardly reticences.

XII.22 ✍ IN LARGER WALLS OF ROMAN BRICKWORK, you will find the rectangular monotony broken up by archlike forms which seem at first glance to connote old entrances, since bricked in. These are supporting arches, a Roman innovation, placed strategically to support the great weight of the wall. Well-ordered memories can do something similar to this in bearing the weight of time, supporting with their forms material which would otherwise fall into chaos. One such form is the keeping of a journal. Journals can serve many purposes — creative, professional, psychological; but no matter why we keep them, they are a boon in locating our vagrant awarenesses within the broader expanse of time. And indeed they can slow time down by reminding us, again and again, of the breadth and fullness of a single day. You can keep a very simple journal — even a one-liner which merely gives the date, your material progress in work or hobby, and any notable detail of the day; or you can undertake more ambitious ones. The main necessities are that you use convenient physical media, keep them handy and give yourself time to write. If you have something important to say, well and good. If not, write about trivia. The act of writing and maintaining continuity has value in itself. And don't be afraid of being trite. Repetition is inevitable; what matters is honesty and the appreciation of detail. So far as audience is concerned, write what will be in effect a letter to some future self, an expression and preservation of your attitudes and concerns.

XII.23 ✍ IN WRITING YOUR JOURNAL GIVE PRIMARY attention to detail; for it is detail which organizes and preserves experience for your future self or some other reader. General statements like "We had a wonderful time" or "It was a dismal morning" make a mockery of the whole procedure, for they evaluate experience without recreating it. I kept long journals from ages ten to twenty-two, chronicling events and describing emotional states, but again and again missing the physical immediacy of experience, the tiny hooks by which experience could have been caught and held. I failed to record how we looked, what we saw, the minor eccentricities of circumstance which gave special character to a day. I ignored these elements not only through lack of training but through misplaced priorities: I mistakenly assumed that one could discuss the heart of things without discussing the surface of things. And now, twenty to thirty years later, 600 pages of journal seem to have been written by some ghost, a voice dogmatic in its exuberance but wholly disembodied from time.

By all means, describe in detail a single day, especially an average day. In mountains of literature and data concerning the past, we have very little which conveys accurately the minute-by-minute progress of life. Had we more of these modest historical commentaries, we could better sense the background against which more important events occurred. Had we such dispatches from our earlier selves, we could better understand the decisions, or lack of decisions, which mystify us in the present.

XII.24 ✍ APRIL 21, 1979 (CARMEL VALLEY). Today, Saturday, I slept till almost 9, trying to recover from the effects of too much running and too little rest. I rested till the sky was the deep blue of a perfect Carmel Valley morning. I ate hot cereal while my mother-in-law prepared to leave after three weeks of helping us here. Then Anthony and I spent the morning together in the sun, leaving the terrace and courtyard only for a brief diplomatic visit to the family who are moving in across the street. At other times Anthony chased a misguided towhee through the house while I ran after him, telling him to stop; and chased his rabbit from corner to corner of its cage with a piece of wood inserted through the wire. I smoked a cigar and sunned, developing my Mediterranean tan, desultorily reading a book about Galileo. I waited for a call from a friend who is flying in from Los Angeles today. When Micha came out of the bedroom after her morning nap with Nicholas, Anthony feigned pregnancy and announced that his child would be named Treeclimber Grudin, shortly afterward renaming him Grudin Mountainclimber. I write this down as the simple stuff of days, disorganized, various yet somehow undifferentiated, so lacking in pattern and causality that even now, at 2:55 P.M., I have trouble remembering what came first. Without my writing here, no single one of these events would remain in memory; in fact, the whole morning would probably recede into the folds of the past, an incremental drop in the bucket of spring. Yet every moment in the rich sunlight with my son had its own abundant reality, its unhurried sweetness and pleasure.

XII.25 ✍ FRANCES YATES (*The Art of Memory*) tells us that classical orators memorized long and complicated speeches in the following way. Early in his career each orator walked through the rooms of some large building, first memorizing the layout, then noting in a fixed sequence the hundreds of architectural details and pieces of furniture contained in each room. Having internalized these physical forms in a specific sequence, he then used them as an arbitrary abstract framework to which he could "attach" the sequential details of a particular speech. A hallway might become a logical transition, a pediment a disclaimer, a couch an accusation. Using these means, the orator could gain a virtue necessary to all good memories: a general mental framework containing niches into which particular data or devices could be fitted.

The preferred model for classical orations was also, among other things, a kind of memory device. The Greek orator Isocrates (436– 338 B.C.) perfected an oratorical structure which was to influence speakers and writers for over 2,000 years. Each Isocratic oration was composed of five major sections — known in Latin as *proemio*, *expositio*, *narratio*, *refutatio* and *exhortatio* — whose order did not deviate. Each of these sections, moreover, had its own beginning, middle and end. These divisions were not merely arbitrary forms; they performed a logical function and appealed to basic psychological needs. Using them, even fledgling orators could locate themselves and maintain their train of thought during long speeches; accomplished orators could extemporize convincingly. Their example suggests a precept which applies to all memory: to remember anything well, we must understand its general structure.

XII.26 🖎 THE RECALLING OF BEAUTIFUL THINGS, whether they are your own experiences or the achievements of others, is a creative act. Simple ideas can be restated by rote; but profound ideas must be recreated by will and imagination.

XII.27 🖎 ROTE MEMORIZATION IS CONDEMNED by many modern educators, yet I know of no art or science that can be learned without this humble practice. There are few basic skills so valuable as the ability to commit miscellaneous material to memory at short notice. This is less an inherited talent than a universal propensity which can be sharpened by repeated effort. To this purpose I propose a double course: the memorization of significant and reasonable things, and the memorization of nonsense. When we memorize reasonable things, we learn reason and memory together. When we memorize nonsense, we put aside the supporting structure of reason, exercise the muscles of memory alone, and prepare ourselves appropriately for the challenges of our nonsensical world.

XII.28 🖎 AS WE GROW OLDER, POSSESSING progressively more past and less future, memory should become a more and more important function of awareness, until it predominantly defines our individual identity. Those of us who respect and develop memory will not, like others, be doomed in old age to a consciousness which is little more than the light husk of present and future. Ideally, moreover, our memory should increasingly amalgamate our individual experience with the experience of the family and the history of culture. For in this expansion of identity lies a major hope of transcending the oppressive boundary of individual death.

XII.29 🖎 AT CERTAIN MOMENTS IN LIFE, prompted by the excitement of some major event, we look ahead in time and think quite simply, "I shall remember this forever." And this awareness in itself seems to change the present experience, to enhance it like some object being lit suddenly from a new side. These are among the very few times that we have direct and honest contact with our future selves. Otherwise we are largely, and in a sense unnecessarily, exiled from our own future. We seldom (as in a kind of mental photograph) review our present circumstances as they might appear to the relatively objective eyes of some future self. When we plan ahead, we plan for goals, specific and disembodied, rather than for future developments of identity or states of mind. For this reason, I believe, we often look back at our own past with some alienation, even disbelief, as though someone else had lived it. The failure to look at things from the future side, and the resultant lack of temporal coherence, are part of what I mean when I say that we are trapped in time. Our freedom lies in an art which is easier to describe than to practice: the willing extension of self into the future. The young Jean-Jacques Rousseau, experiencing a particularly happy period in his life and fearful lest this happiness should soon fade, decided (as he later put it) to provide himself with talents against the future.* The aim of his studies was not success in the world but rather the creation of an inner world; he sought to fortify, enrich and complete a future state of mind. The young Charles Darwin, as he wandered through the jungle on his first field trips in South America, sensed that the happy confusion of surprise and delight he then enjoyed would someday settle in his mind as intelligible and coherent memory.† Through this multiple awareness, he was able to enjoy the present as past, present and future in one. These are both examples of a heroic view of time — a dignity which, by refusing to be limited by the present, paradoxically endows the present with unexcelled volume and richness. For in extending our being into the future, we give new significance to present action, and in reviewing the present as future memory we help make it memorable.

XII.30 ✑ ONE DAY IN JANUARY 1977, I TOOK MY son Anthony out on a constitutional into nearby Hendricks Park.

---

* Rousseau, *Les Reveries du Promeneur Solitaire* (1778), final sentence.
† See Darwin, *Diary of the Voyage of HMS Beagle*, ed. Nora Barlow (Cambridge University Press, 1934), p. 39.

Anthony, who at nine months of age much delighted in these excursions, was bundled into a package of clothing about twice his size, stuffed with difficulty into a backpack and hefted off by me up the road and into the big grove of Douglas fir. That day we had the kind of weather we get in Oregon only once or twice a year: a great mist, heavy and dank and pure from the distant ocean, covered even the tallest hills; but above and beyond the mist there was nothing remotely watery for 90 million miles up to the sun, which would in hours provide a mild and brilliant day. Walking unhurriedly through the hilltop park, I could see in the branches high above me swirls of gold which heralded the good weather to come. I had been having a difficult winter. My future livelihood at that point depended on a single large and sloppy pile of pages whose contents so far had left its official readers undecided between distaste and outrage. My colleagues at the university had little to say to me — not from unfriendliness but rather from the embarrassment generated by a fellow worker who has profoundly and stubbornly erred in his labors. But that morning, as I strolled with my delighted son in the cold fog which was itself so delightfully promising, I felt a weird visitation of joy; as though the conglomerate symbols of futurity — mist verging on sunlight, morning on day, babyhood on boyhood, winter on spring — all suggeested the imminent sweeping in of a storm of happiness. I cannot think of this event, even though it is now long past, without being palpably reminded of the future; and I mean the future not in its usual sense as an indefinite field of will and circumstance, but as a spiritual presence, a pure intimation of latent fullness and joy. Paradoxically, I carry the future better in memory than in any other aspect of awareness.

XIII ⚘ THE MUSIC OF
MEN'S LIVES ⚘ ⚘ ⚘ ⚘

XIII.1 ⚘ FREYA STARK, REMEMBERING HER maternal grandmother:

> She carried about her that best of grandmotherly atmospheres — a sense of amplitude in Time. No hurry ever came near her. A whole series of episodes in my childhood show her peacefully reading, or dressing, or brushing the long white hair that could still touch her knees, while a babel of agitated voices urged departing carriages or trains. She always had a book in her hand and never seemed busy; she would put it down and her arms would open to enclose any human being, but particularly a child, who needed refuge there; what she gave was affection pure and simple, deliberately free from wear and tear of understanding or advice.*

Love, which more than any other emotion exists in all four dimensions, is impossible without the gift of time. It cannot exist amid haste and confusion; or between people who parcel their affection into short periods. The most impassioned actions and assurances, when punctuated by days of coldness or distraction, are as puny in their own way as limp handshakes and pats on the head. We love only when we love across time, when love offered is love remembered and love promised.

XIII.2 ⚘ THIS MORNING I NOTICED THAT THE cover of one of these two big Spanish notebooks (this manuscript)

---

* Stark, *Traveller's Prelude* (Baltimore: Penguin, 1962).

is breaking at the rings and threatening to fall off altogether within two or three more months of use. Such insignificant portents are of desperate urgency to a writer, who tends to view the physical paraphernalia of his work with much the same impassioned regard as that of a sea captain toward the decks and bulwarks of his vessel. If one of these notebooks falls apart before I have finished this stage of my work, I must either buy a new notebook and set it up with the appropriate headings (which would be rather like leaving my wife for a high school cheerleader) or set about transferring 60,000 words of manuscript into an entirely new format. Neither alternative is attractive. These soiled and ratty notebooks do not just hold my work, they *are* my work. My eyes and hands appreciate the soft and shaggy quality which my use has given them; they are swollen as if pregnant with earnest ink; their increasing fullness with particolored henscratch approximates my own character more and more each day. I would rather spend hours patching them than give them up.

More generally I am fascinated by the idea of objects grown old with gentle use (my pipes, my shoes, my yellowed shaving brush, even my power lawnmower) or maltreated and discarded objects (houses, cars, furniture) which I can acquire and restore to heartiness. I cannot fully explain my love of such things, but opine that it is because they symbolize the ability of matter and spirit to float gracefully in time, to bend with time at its own curve, to wrinkle, soften, fade, but survive so much the more intact. And this unique preservation of essence, born of care, patience and enduring respect, is even more beautiful when it occurs in human relationships and things of the mind.

XIII.3 ✒ THE PHYSICAL IMMEDIACY OF THE present — its insistent, almost sluttish availability — tends to blind us to its more spiritual identity, which is unique and fragile and doomed. The present is like a doomed princess, elegant and inexpressibly beautiful, burning out her close of life in the guise of a hoyden. She is always ours to take, yet we accept this invitation all too seldom; and even accepting it we seldom realize that we have not made a minor material conquest but rather come into contact with a sovereign spirit, entered a realm of being whose light and power transfigure all the other elements. Most often, we refuse her offer, perhaps because her ascendant sister beckons (with features ingeniously adorned by the lights and shadows of the future), perhaps because we are tired or fearful, perhaps because she seems so almost distastefully available. And most likely this is but one link in a whole long chain of refusals, one step in a lifelong journey against the grain of time.

XIII.4 ✒ HAPPINESS (AS SUGGESTED, FOR EXAMPLE, by the French word for happy, *heureux*) may well consist primarily of an attitude toward time. Individuals we consider happy commonly seem *complete in the present:* we see them constantly in their wholeness, attentive, cheerful, open rather than closed to events, integral in the moment rather than distended across time by regret or anxiety. Yet paradoxically they give an impression of permanence and consistency. They do not change greatly from day to day. They choose and patiently develop lengthy projects, so voluminous in time that the work of a single day is no more than a strand in the weft of a rug. They love remembering past experiences and making plans; they speak of past and future, not as external contexts, but rather as esteemed confederates, quiet extensions of their own being. One almost feels that their lives possess a kind of qualified eternity: that past and future, birth and death, meet for them as in the completion of a circle.

XIII.5 ✒ A MAN MADE A LONG PILGRIMAGE TO A holy city. As he neared the city he saw, looming above the lower irregular shapes of other structures, the walls and roof of the great temple that was the object of his journey. Yet again and again, as he searched through dark narrow alleys and small marketplaces, he failed to find its entrance. As best he could, in a language not his own, he made inquiries of the townspeople; but all of them, taught in a newer religion, seemed neither to know nor to care. After much frustration, he was directed at last to a priest of the old faith, who told him that the great temple had in fact long ceased to possess a formal entrance, but rather could be entered in many ways, through any of a large number of the narrow houses and tiny shops which surrounded it. Yet in the end this revelation gave the pilgrim no help at all. Each house or shop he entered seemed so dark and squalid, its furniture so alien, its occupants so forbidding, that it seemed manifestly incapable of opening into the grandeur and freedom of the temple vault. The man left the city in bitterness and sought an easier faith.

≱ *POSTSCRIPT* ≱

For encouragement, support and counsel received during and after the composition of this book, I wish to thank the following people: Helen Beck, Ray Birn, Harry and Muriel Bowker, Jan Broekhoff, Richard Maxwell Brown, George Carroll, Sarah Christensen, Pat Crain, Henry and Vergilia Dakin, Paula De Young, Frank Duveneck, James Earl, Lowell Edmunds, Ruth Edwards, Mel Erickson, Edward and Nana Faridany, John H. Finley, Jr., Lilian Furst, Stanley and Thelma Greenfield, Gwilym Griffith-Jones, Eva and Peter Grudin, Ruth Grudin, Pat Hardisty, James and Rosalie Heacock, Cindy Heidemann, David Hill, Seymour House, Jeffrey Hurwit, David Jensen, Katrina Kenison, Rodney Kilcup, Gregory Knecht, Joseph Lawrence, Joachim and Marianne Leppmann, Steven Lewers, Doris Little, Peter Little, Val Lorwin, John Loudon, Richard Lucas, Letitia Lynn, Lee McCarthy, Christina Melk, Michael Menaker, Carlisle Moore, Michael Moravcsik, Nancy Morrow, Helen and Peter Neumeyer, Frederick Newberry, John Nicols, Dorothea Oppenheimer, John and Maria Paasche, Joan and Stanley Pierson, Charles and Charlotte Poletti, Jeffrey Porter, Elizabeth and Peter Raby, Jim Sanderson, Martha Sherwood, Elizabeth Sifton, W. Sherwin Simmons, Hans and Margit Speier, Jane and Richard Stevenson, Charlotte Sullivan, David Sweet, Dominic Valiunes, Jandina Watrud, Barbara von Websky, George Wickes and Barbara Zukin. I am indebted also to the Carmel Public Library, the Carmel Valley Public Library, the Huntington Library and the Library of the University of Oregon. The Graduate School and the Provost's Office of the University of Oregon awarded grants which aided me in completing the project, and the office staff of the English Department gave extremely effective help. To my parents, Abraham and Bertha Grudin, and to my wife, Michaela, I wish to express my gratitude and love.